Traditional Quilts with a TWIST

MAGGIE BALL

Published by

700 East State Street • Iola, WI 54990-0001
715-445-2214 • 888-457-2873

Our toll-free number to place an order or obtain a free catalog is (800) 258-0929.

Library of Congress Catalog Number 2006922398

ISBN-13: 978-0-89689-273-6
ISBN-10: 0-89689-273-5

Designed by Emily Adler and Marilyn McGrane
Edited by Candy Wiza and Annette Gentry Bailey

Printed in China

Dedication

To Selenge, my Mongolian friend and quilting colleague. Your determination and perseverance is amazing and inspiring.

Acknowledgments

I'd like to express my appreciation to those who have guided and assisted me throughout creating this book. Many thanks are given to all, especially the following:

The Krause Publications team for the book production, notably, Julie Stephani and Candy Wiza.

David Textiles Inc., for generously providing fabric for many of the quilts.

Joe and Mary Koval, for the loan of their antique quilts featured at the start of each project section.

The Electric Quilt Company, for computer software that was a tremendous tool when designing projects and preparing material for the Krause Publications illustrator, Emily Adler.

Marcia Barrett, Joanne Bennett, Susan Burker, Heather Coats, Deborah Haynes, Linda Johnston, Valerie Martinson, Barbara Michael and Gladys Schulz for graciously sharing their beautiful quilts.

Mark Frey, for a fantastic job photographing all the quilts that we couldn't send to Krause Publications.

Wanda Rains, for her outstanding machine-quilting skills, friendship and good humor throughout the whole endeavor.

My husband, Nigel, who played a vital role as my computer guru and the provider of constant love and support.

Table of Contents

Introduction

Many traditional quilt patterns have stood the test of time with flying colors, despite the changing trends in available fabrics and new quilting techniques. We twist and tweak the traditional patterns just by making our own unique fabric choices. Even a very simple pattern, such as a nine-patch, may be reproduced in numerous ways with different value placements, colors and settings. As a teacher, I love to see the fabrics that my students select and the variety of quilts that emerge from the same starting point. Many of today's award-winning quilts retain a strong traditional flavor, but at the same time, have progressed dynamically from the original blocks and settings.

My quilting has strong traditional roots. I began quilting in 1986 when I moved to Arkansas and saw beautiful quilts in traditional patterns for sale, hanging on washing lines and picket fences in the Ozarks. I took classes to learn to piece the well-loved blocks and was intrigued by how different they looked when I changed the values and settings. This fascination continues to influence my work, and many of my quilts contain strong traditional elements. I twist and tweak patterns in a variety of ways. This gallery contains a selection of my work and illustrates some of the many possibilities.

Traditional blocks in an unusual setting

Celestial Garden designed and pieced by the author, machine quilted by Wanda Rains, 2002 (84" x 84") Photo by Mark Frey

Medallion style with a variety of patterns

Wedding Quilt designed and pieced by the author, machine quilted by Wanda Rains, 2001 (82" x 82") Photo by Mark Frey

Alternate two different blocks to create a secondary pattern

Kaleidoscopic Garden designed, pieced and hand quilted by the author, 1994 (80" x 80") Photo by Mark Frey

Rearrange units within blocks

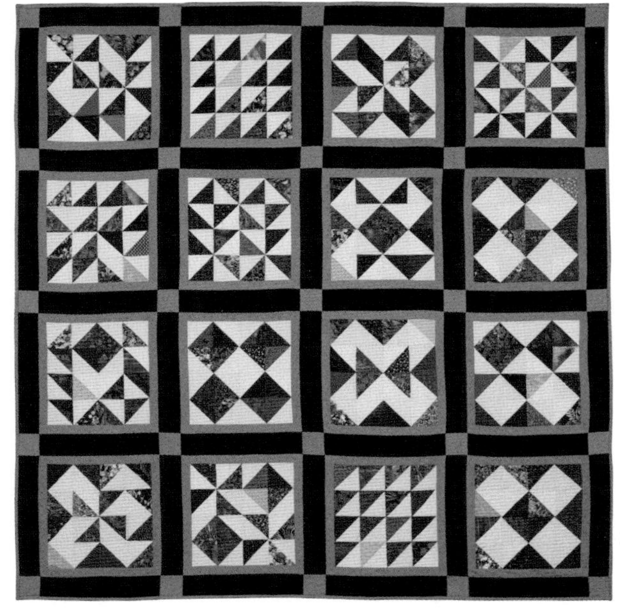

Patchwork Geometry project designed by the author, blocks designed by children at The Family Classroom, Bainbridge Island Alternative School, pieced by the author, Mavis Tullis and Wanda Rains, machine quilted by Tammy Stoll, 1997 (69" x 69") Photo by Mark Frey

Distort width and length of blocks to create illusion of curves

I Love Pansies designed, pieced and hand quilted by the author, 1995 (41" x 41")

Insert sashing between blocks

Blogs 2003 made by the author, 2003 (41" x 41")

Adaptation of a traditional pattern, Mongolian Ölzii, not previously used in quilting

Tribute to Mongolia designed and pieced by the author, machine quilted by Wanda Rains, 2004 (103" x 103") Photo by Mark Frey

In this book, I present variations of three of my personal favorite quilt patterns: Trip Around the World, Ohio Star and Bear's Paw. These patterns, like many others, are versatile and lend themselves well to twisting. For Trip Around the World, most of the patterns plug pieced blocks into the Trip Around the World format, and some have sashing between the blocks. The Ohio Star appears in a variety of sizes, with a lattice inserted, and as an altered block with extra triangles and a pieced frame. In the Bear's Paw, I substitute the four large squares for pieced sections to create new blocks. There are a variety of projects for each pattern type, ranging from small wall hangings to large queen-sized bed quilts; and from easy to challenging in skill requirements. I hope that you'll be inspired by the book and enjoy twisting and tweaking traditional patterns in your own special way.

CHAPTER ONE

How to Use this Book

The book begins with an overview of what you'll find in each chapter. Chapter Two contains a comprehensive review of quilting basics. You'll find full instructions for all the piecing techniques used in the projects as well as guidelines for making your quilt from start to finish. Use this for help with completing your projects, from fabric selection to attaching the binding. Beginning quilters should find this chapter especially useful.

The projects follow, and are grouped according to the traditional pattern from which they are derived:

Chapter Three: Trip Around the World

Chapter Four: Ohio Star

Chapter Five: Bear's Paw

In general, the patterns become more challenging as you advance through the book. Chapter Three contains quick and easy projects and is the best starting place for beginners. Accuracy of piecing becomes more important with the increased frequency of triangles in the Ohio Star and Bear's Paw patterns. Each project is ranked according to the level of difficulty (easy, average and challenging), and some are clearly far more labor intensive than others. There are a variety of project sizes, from small quilts and tote bags, to large queen-sized quilts.

As you begin quilt construction, keep in mind the following:

- Use a consistent ¼" seam allowance.
- The term "full-width" refers to 42" wide fabric.
- The fabric requirements are given for the sample quilts shown with extra to allow for errors.
- If you change the pattern or the number of fabrics, you'll need to adjust the fabric quantities.
- Read through all the directions for a project before beginning.

This book is a springboard for your imagination. Feel free to make any substitutions and design modifications. Ideas for tweaking are given in "Suggestions for Twisting and Tweaking Traditional Quilts." Have fun and enjoy making the projects!

SUGGESTIONS FOR TWISTING AND TWEAKING TRADITIONAL QUILTS

Rearrange the units within blocks.
Use unusual value placements to accentuate blocks in new ways.
Combine areas within blocks to simplify.
Subdivide units within blocks, making the patterns more complex.
Introduce a lattice (narrow grid) within blocks.
Overlap blocks or create blocks within blocks.
Slash blocks and insert strips or pieced sections (confidence is essential).
Distort blocks, lengthening and/or widening them (challenging).
Alternate two different blocks.
Use a combination of several different blocks.
Use color or value to create secondary patterns extending across the blocks and/or to make one large pattern.
Replicate blocks — or parts of them — in a different size elsewhere in the quilt.
Create new and unusual settings for traditional blocks.
Insert sashing, which may be pieced, between blocks that are traditionally adjacent.
Extend the blocks or parts of them into the border of the quilt.
Embellish the quilt with beads, couching, buttons or anything you like.
Use computer software to help you design and play.

CHAPTER TWO

Quilting Basics

You'll need several tools and supplies before beginning your projects. In addition, you'll want to understand fabric selection and planning, rotary cutting, piecing techniques, and more. Read on for all of the details.

Tools and Supplies

Here is a list of useful quilting supplies for the projects in this book. If you are a new quilter, you can gradually acquire items as you need them. The most timesaving and essential tools, after the sewing machine, are the rotary cutter used with a cutting mat and a 6" x 24" quilters' ruler.

- Sewing machine in good working order
- Iron and ironing board
- 45mm rotary cutter
- 17" x 23" cutting mat, minimum size
- 6" x 24" quilters' ruler
- 15" x 15" square ruler
- 6" x 6" square ruler
- 12" ruler
- Sewing scissors
- Paper cutting scissors
- Graph paper
- Small sticky labels
- Locking plastic bags for storage
- Mechanical pencil with fine lead (0.5 mm)
- Variety of 100-percent cotton fabrics (flannel optional)
- Batting
- Quilting hoop and thimble (for hand quilting)
- Needles and pins
- Thread
- Decorative threads
- Old dessert spoon
- Marking pencils or chalk pencils
- T-pins for basting
- Safety pins
- Seam ripper
- Masking tape

If you are fortunate enough to have a permanent quilting area in your home, I highly recommend a work wall. A work wall can be made with a piece of batting or the backside of a vinyl tablecloth. Simply tape it to the wall and place your pieces or blocks on the wall to view your design. It works well for previewing the quilt top and making changes, if desired.

Fabric Selection and Planning

Choose fabrics that you like. Your choice will personalize your quilt and make it unique. If you don't know where to begin, try choosing a multi-colored print (which could be a theme print) then pick out matching colors in a variety of values. You don't have to make all your choices before you begin. Often, I make my quilt blocks or the center of a quilt before I decide which fabrics to use in the sashing strips and borders. Once the blocks are completed, I audition different fabrics to see which ones I like the best. You may take your blocks to a store to test them with a variety of fabrics. Color, value, and print scale are all important factors to consider. The most successful quilts are often the ones with the most variety.

Quilters generally use 100-percent cotton fabrics and wash them before sewing. Plan your project, being realistic about your skill level and time available. Make notes to help you stay organized. Draw a sketch with annotations so that you know the positions of the different fabrics. Record the sizes of the pieces to be cut (don't forget to include the ¼" seam allowances) and the number needed for each fabric. If you run out of a particular fabric, you may have to improvise with other fabrics or include extra pieced sections. (Sometimes, this can lead you along a more creative path, so it's not always a bad thing.)

To estimate yardage, work out how many pieces of the required size will fit across one width of fabric (standard fabric width is 42"). Calculate the number of strips you'll need to cut, and hence the total length of fabric needed. (Allow yourself some extra fabric in case of errors.) Border strips require long pieces of fabric unless you plan to piece them (see page 28). Quilt backs may need two or more full lengths of fabric if the quilt is wider than 42". They may be pieced from project leftovers, or made from wider fabric (see page 29). To calculate the amount of fabric needed for binding, measure the perimeter of the quilt and work out how many full-width 2½" strips to cut. If you have trouble making estimates, quilt store staff should be able to assist you. Don't be afraid to ask for help if you need it.

Fabric Basics

When cutting fabric, pay attention to the direction of the grain. (Grain is the way that the fabric is woven.)

FABRIC BASICS, GRAIN DIRECTION

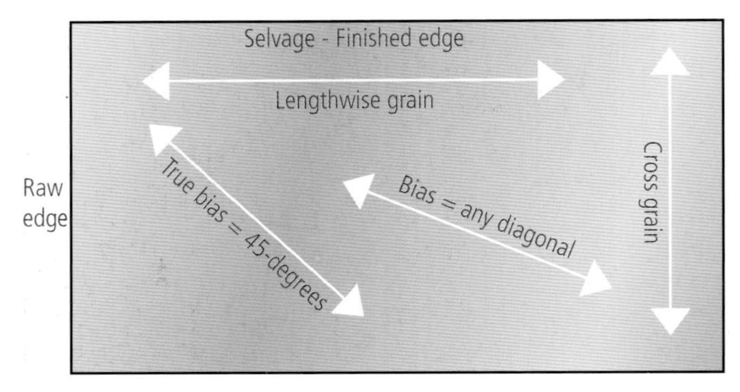

The term "straight-of-grain" refers to both the lengthwise and cross grains. Bias edges stretch and easily become misshapen, so patchwork pieces are usually cut with as many sides as possible aligned with the straight-of-grain. Check that the outer edges of quilt blocks are on the straight-of-grain to reduce distortion. Cut strips, squares and rectangles in alignment with the grain unless they are being fussy-cut for a particular motif in the fabric. Obviously, right-angled triangles have to have at least one bias edge. If the long side of the triangle is on the outer edge of the block, then the triangle will have two bias edges. Do not use the selvages.

On some fabrics, especially solid colors and batiks, it's hard to tell the right side from the wrong side. If you can't tell, then don't be concerned about it. There is no reason why you shouldn't use the back of a fabric as the "right" side, if desired.

Rotary Cutting Fabric

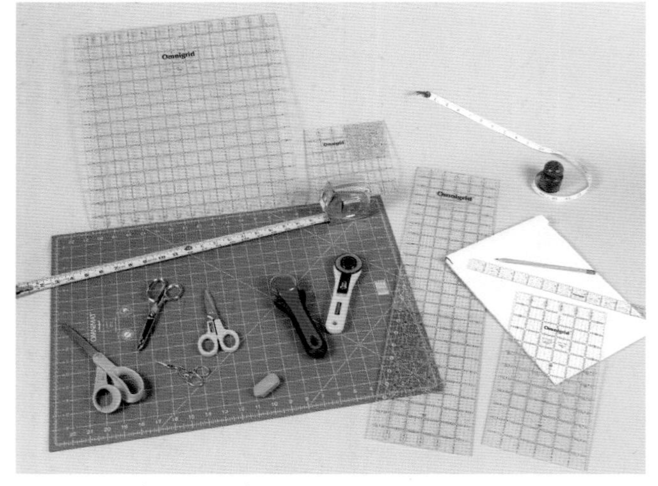

Measuring and cutting tools
Photo by Mark Frey

Rotary cutters are wonderful timesaving cutting tools. I recommend 45mm rotary cutters, mats of a minimum size of 17" x 23", and Omnigrid rulers. Most of the time I use the 6" x 24" ruler. The 15" square is useful for cutting pieces wider than 6"; and the 6" square is excellent for trimming half- or quarter-square triangle units.

Never allow the rotary cutter to leave your hand with the blade exposed. I cannot emphasize this enough. Always retract the blade, even if you are going to pick up the cutter again to make another cut (who knows, you may be interrupted). Make a habit of closing the blade before you put it down, or use the type of cutter that automatically retracts its blade. Follow these steps to cut fabric accurately.

1 Press the fabric.

2 Fold the fabric selvage to selvage. You may find that the raw edge has not been cut straight; make the fold so the fabric will lie flat.

3 Fold the fabric again in the same direction, and place it flat on the cutting mat with the selvage edges at the top. You now have four layers of fabric.

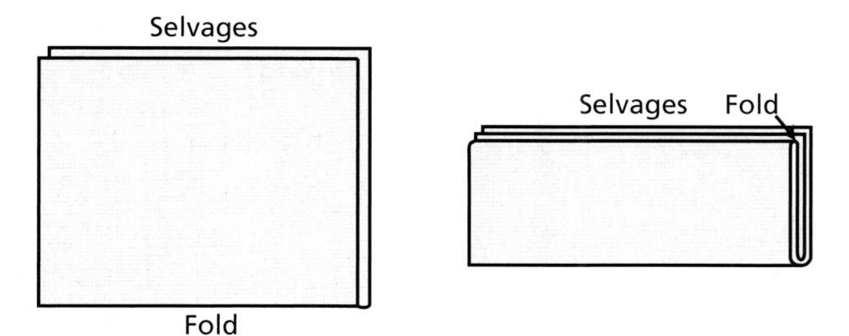

4 Cut to straighten the raw edge. Line up a horizontal line on your 6" x 24" ruler with the fold at the bottom of the fabric. Move the ruler as close as possible to the raw edge of the fabric so there is minimum waste, but so that the raw edges on the layers of fabric are exposed. Hold the ruler firmly in position with one hand. Hold the cutter as you would a sharp knife, your forefinger extended and the shaft upright with the blade flush against the ruler. Apply some downward pressure and cut in one motion away from your body, keeping the blade next to the edge of the ruler. Maintaining the position of the ruler, remove the raw edge you just cut. If the cut did not penetrate all the layers, repeat the cut with your ruler still in place.

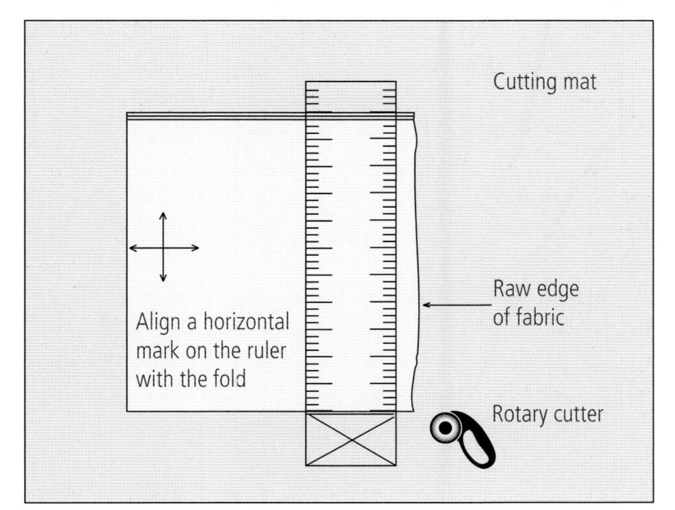

Cut to straighten the raw edge.

5 To make the next cut, carefully rotate the fabric without disturbing the straight edge, or move around the table to the opposite side of the cutting board. Cut strips the desired width, using a ruler. If your original cut was not straight, or the ruler slipped on the second cut, you'll no longer have parallel sides on the strip and may have angles or so-called "doglegs" on the folds. Straighten the edge and repeat the steps

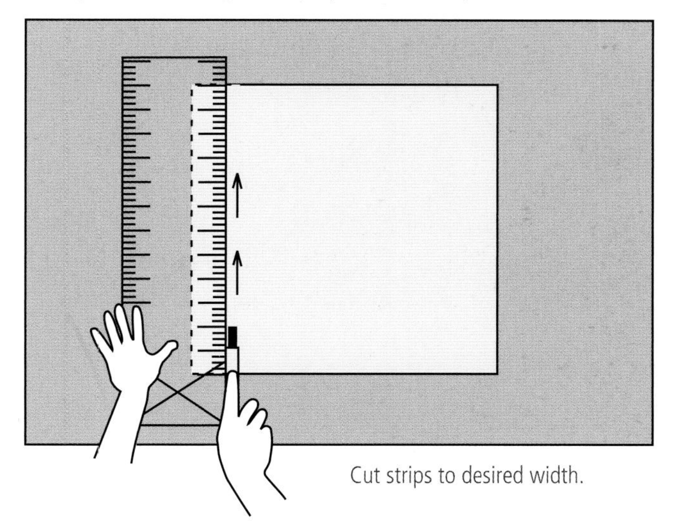

Cut strips to desired width.

6 Counter-cut strips to make pieces the desired size. Note: Counter-cut means to cut the opposite direction previously cut.

7 To cut strips or squares larger than 6", use a large square ruler or measure from the grid of the cutting mat. Cut the pieces large enough to include the ¼" seam allowance on each side. For example, a 4" square should be cut 4½" square to allow ¼" on each side and a 3" x 5" rectangle should be cut 3½" x 5½".

TIPS:

Always close the blade on the rotary cutter when it leaves your hand.

Replace the blade when it becomes dull.

When making multiple cuts, check that the raw edge remains square. If it is skewed, trim to straighten before making the next cut.

Take time to cut precisely to ensure accurately sized pieces.

Machine Piecing Techniques

Sew patchwork pieces together with a ¼" seam allowance, unless otherwise instructed. Use a ¼" foot on the machine, or adjust the position of the needle to make the accurate ¼" seam allowance. Being consistent and precise will make your piecing much easier, especially when you construct patchwork in a variety of sizes. Plan the order of piecing so that you always sew in straight lines and avoid insetting corners. (All the quilts in this book may be pieced without any insetting; backstitching is only used when mitering corners on borders.)

The finished size is the measurements of a completed piece, block or quilt top without the seam allowances. When we refer to 9" or 12" quilt blocks, this is the finished size. The unfinished size is the measurements of a completed piece, block or quilt top raw edge to raw edge, before assembly. The unfinished size includes the seam allowance. The unfinished sizes of 9" and 12" blocks are 9½" and 12½", respectively.

Pinning, Pressing and Assembly Line Sewing

Use of pins will stabilize the pieces as you sew. Place them perpendicular to the sewing line with the heads extending ¼" to ½" beyond the raw edges so that they may be removed easily. I always pin at the intersections of pieced sections where the seams abut, when sewing bias edges together and for adding border strips.

Pinning is important when piecing units with triangles and helps avoid blunt or floating points. The area around triangle points is usually thick from the seam allowances and difficult to pin. Match up the triangle points exactly and stick a pin straight down through them to stabilize. Then add a pin on either side; remove the vertical pin.

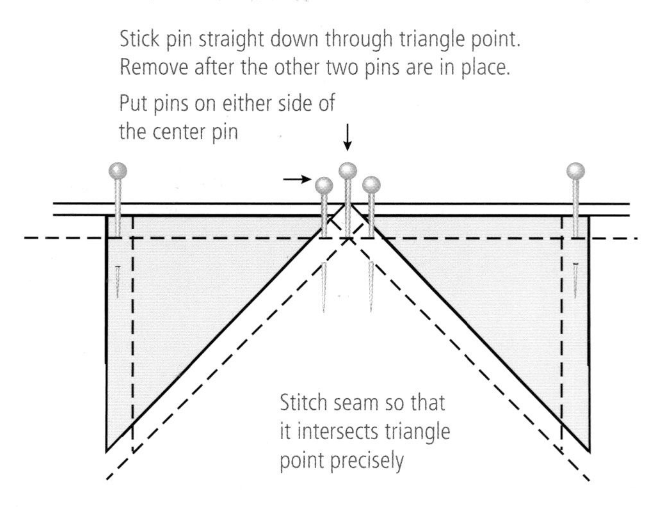

If your cutting or piecing is inaccurate and you are unable to correct it, you may need to ease in extra amounts of fabric when you join two pieces. Pin so that the excess is distributed evenly along the seam length. Do this by pinning the ends and centers together first, then halfway between the center and the end, and so on. If the longer of the fabrics is placed on the underside when you machine sew, it will be easier to accommodate the excess. When working with two pieced sections, pin all the seam intersections first to make sure they are in the correct position. Then, if necessary, add more pins in between.

To press, use the iron on the hot cotton setting. I like to use steam. In general, seam allowances are pressed to one side, toward the darkest fabric. If possible, try to press so that the seams of pieced sections abut in opposite directions; for example when sewing rows of squares or blocks together. In some cases, where several seam allowances intersect, such as the eight triangle points in the center of a pinwheel, seams may be pressed open to reduce the bulk.

Assembly-line piecing saves time and thread and enables you to sew the pieces from edge to edge. You can machine piece several units of fabric together one after another without lifting the presser foot or cutting the threads between the units. Start by sewing on a small scrap of fabric folded in half. (I refer to this as the spacer strip.) Then feed in the patchwork pieces. If you make a habit of sewing on the spacer strip every time you complete each batch of piecing, you'll always be ready to start sewing again.

Strip-Piecing

Strip-piecing is a technique in which strips of fabric are cut and then joined lengthwise. The joined strips may then be counter-cut to make units for the quilt. Not only does this create accurate-sized pieces, it saves time — especially when multiple strips or large numbers of four-patch and nine-patch units are involved.

It takes two strips to make four-patch units. Press seams toward darker fabric so that seams abut at intersection.

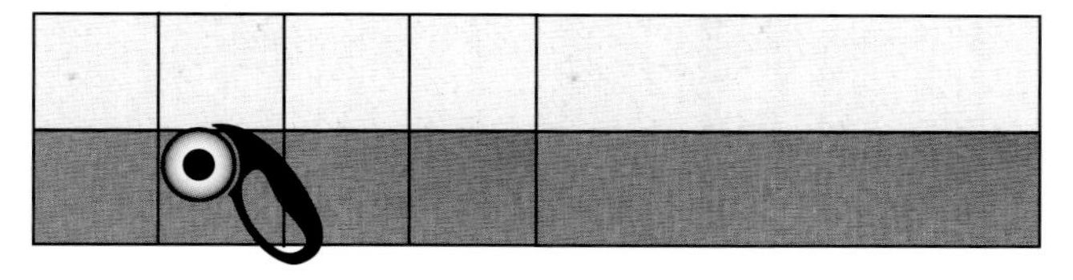

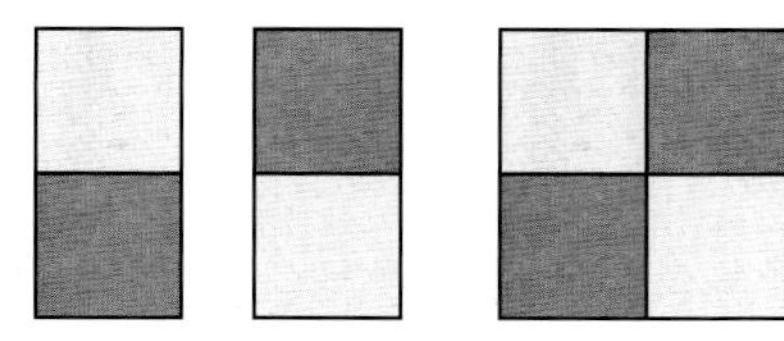

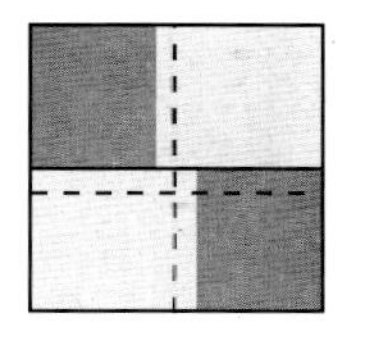

Backside showing abutting seams

It takes two sets of three strips to make nine-patch units. Press seams toward darker fabrics so that seams abut on backside.

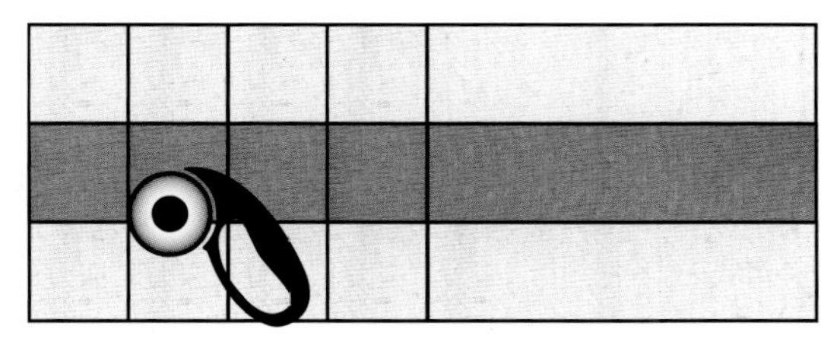

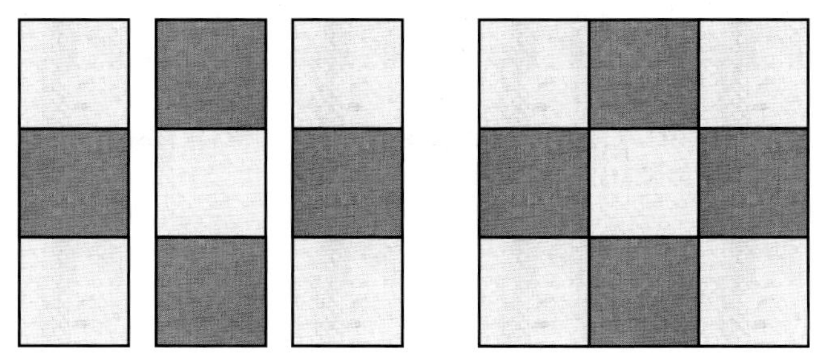

Corner-Square Triangles

In this technique, bias edges of triangular pieces are sewn together before cutting on the bias. The triangles are accurate and easy to make.

To make corner-square triangles, cut squares and mark them on the wrong side with a diagonal line, corner to corner, using a fine mechanical pencil (0.5 mm lead). Sew along the marked line when you attach them to larger squares or rectangles. Once the seam is stitched, trim away the excess seam allowance, and then press the seam allowance toward the darkest fabric. The corner-square triangle differs from the half-square triangle, in that each square only yields one triangle and you sew on the marked diagonal line. In this book, corner-square triangles are used in the Bowtie, Sawtooth Star, Tweaked Ohio Star blocks and in some of the Bear's Paw variations.

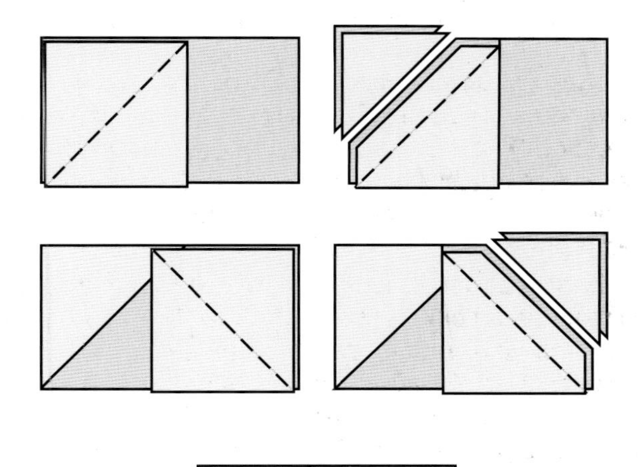

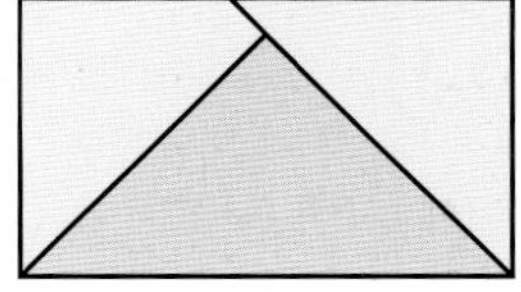

Create star points using the corner-square triangle method.
Star points - two corner triangles sewn onto a rectangle

Half-Square Triangles

Half-square triangles are triangles made by dividing squares in half diagonally. The long sides of these right-angled triangles are bias edges. In this method of piecing, the triangles are joined into squares without cutting the bias edge until after the seam has been sewn. Squares are cut and sewn, not triangles. Cut a square of each of the two triangle fabrics ⅞" larger than the finished size of the square unit you want to make (to allow for the seam allowances around the triangles). Draw a diagonal line from corner to corner on the backside of the lighter of the two squares using a fine mechanical pencil (0.5 mm lead). Sew the two squares right sides together with two ¼" seams — one on each side of the line. Cut along the center pencil line and open up the pieced squares. Each set of squares yields two half-square triangle units. Press the seam allowance toward the darkest fabric.

Make half-square triangles.

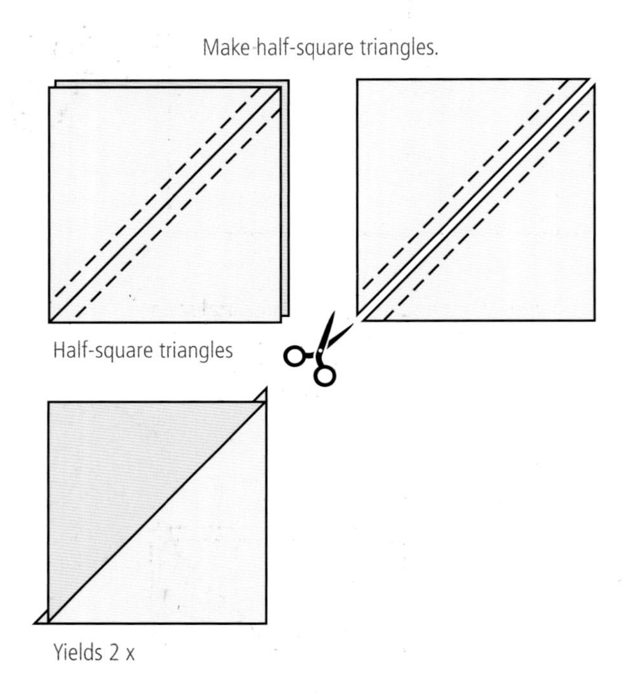

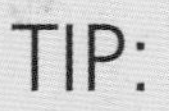

Yields 2 x

Trim half-square triangles.

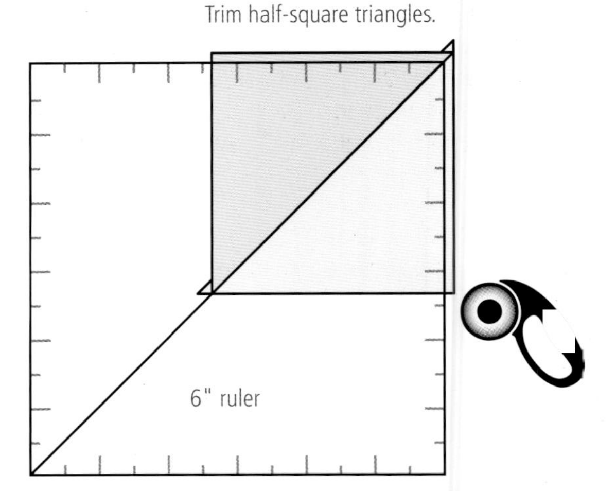

Align diagonal line on 6" ruler with diagonal seam line. Trim the two sides so that the unit remains larger than the required size.

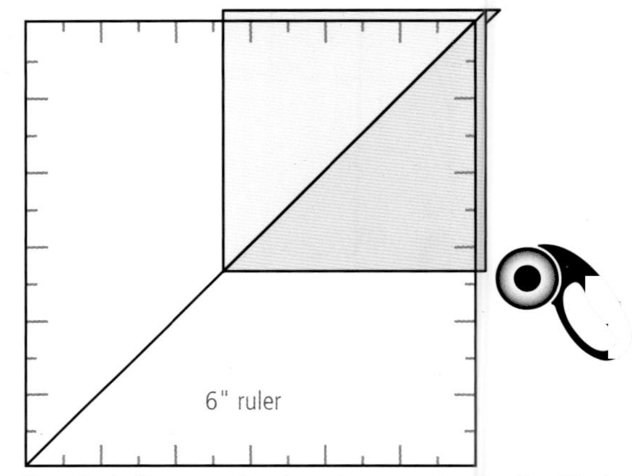

Turn the half-square triangle and once again align the 6" ruler with the seam line. Cut the unit to the exact size required.

This technique also makes cutting the original squares easier, by avoiding the necessity to cut in eighths of inches. The trimming takes a little time, but the end product is worth the effort and fits perfectly with the other patchwork pieces.

TIP:

To make accurate half-square triangles, cut the original squares 1" larger than the finished size of the square unit desired. Using a 6" square ruler, trim the half-square triangle units to the precise size, being careful to maintain the triangle points in the corners. Align the diagonal line on the ruler with the seam line between the triangles and trim a little off all four sides to create a perfectly square unit. All the half-square triangles in the featured projects were made in this way.

Quarter-Square Triangles

Quarter-square triangles are square units divided diagonally both ways into four triangles. Begin by making half-square triangle units as described on page 16. Cut them in half diagonally and then join them in the appropriate pairs to make the quarter-square triangle units.

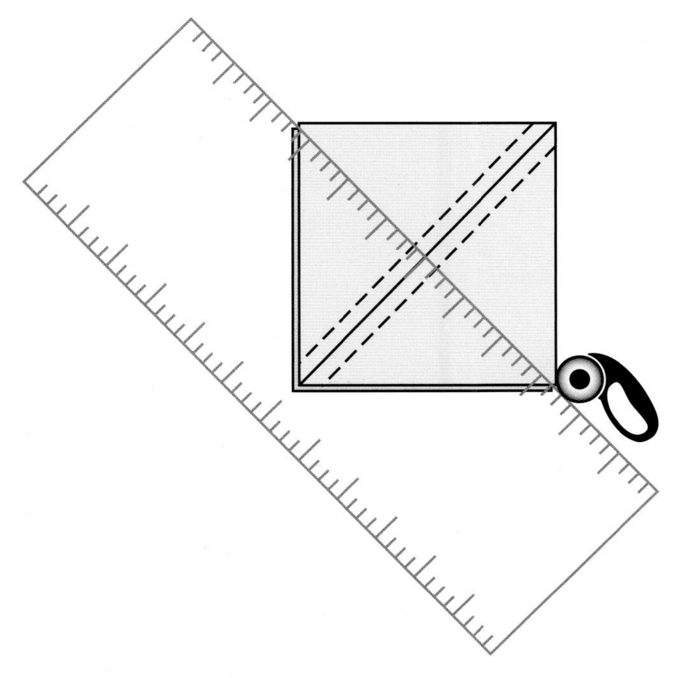

Cut in half diagonally as shown, and then cut along the diagonal pencil lines.

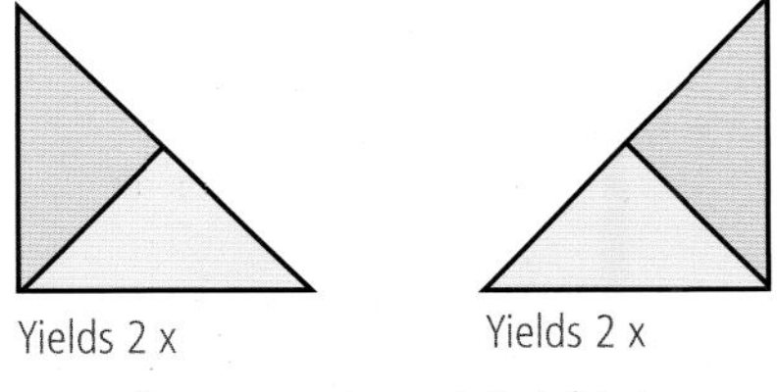

Press seams toward dark fabric.

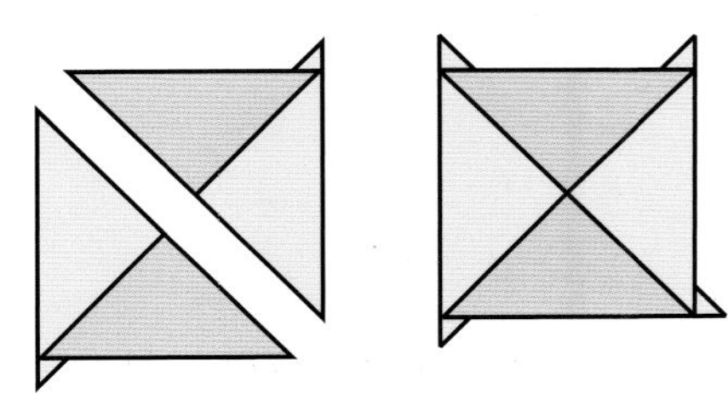

Join triangles in pairs to complete the units.

This time, the original squares should be cut 1¼" larger than the finished square unit (to allow for the seam allowances around the triangles). Use a scant ¼" seam allowance; piece and trim each side to make the unit precise. Be careful to maintain all the points and to cut so that the center intersection is exactly in the middle. For example, when trimming a unit to 3" the central point should be 1½" from all sides.

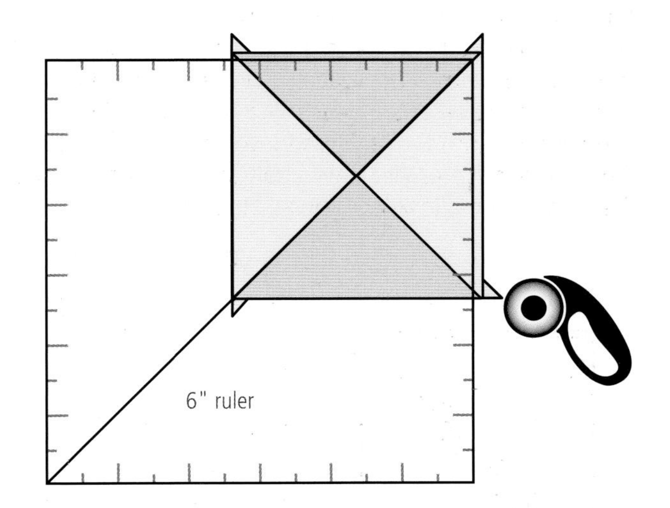

Align diagonal line on 6" ruler with diagonal seam line and central intersection with half of the unit size, i.e., for a 3" unit; center intersection should be 1½" from both edges of the ruler. Trim two sides.

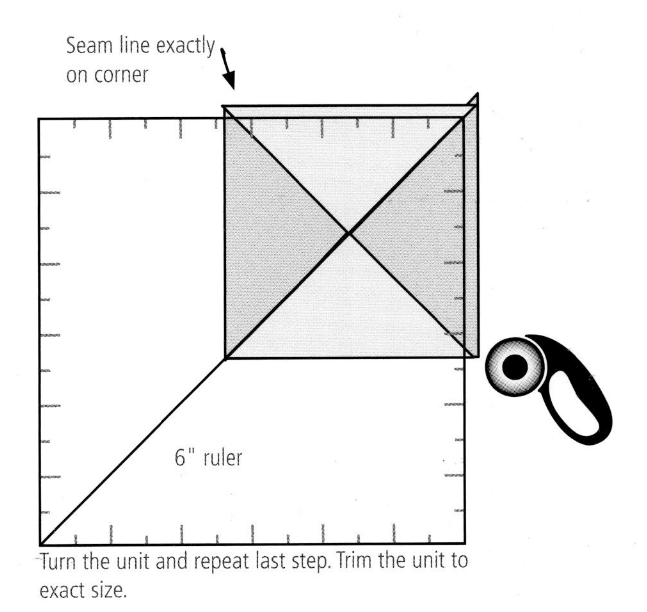

Turn the unit and repeat last step. Trim the unit to exact size.

Block Construction

For ease of piecing, sew in straight lines and avoid insetting corners. Most quilt blocks may be divided into square units of equal sizes — for example, the four-patch, nine-patch and 16-patch. The square units may, or may not, be further subdivided. Begin by piecing all these units and then arrange them into the correct configuration. Join them together in rows, and then assemble the rows.

Here are step-by-step guides for piecing common blocks found in the projects. Cutting sizes are provided in the project instructions.

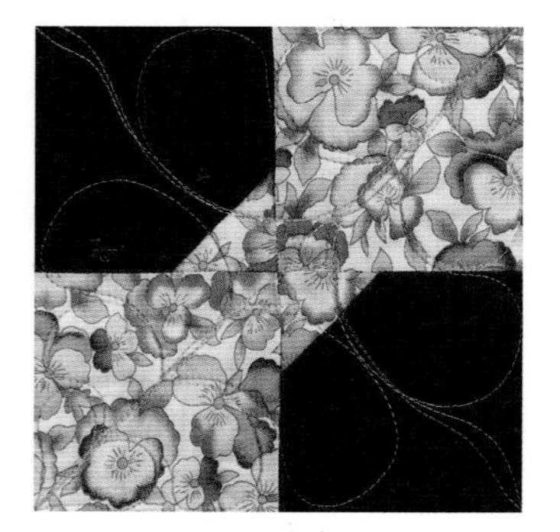

Bowtie Blocks

Use the corner-square triangle method (see page15) to sew the small triangles onto one corner of each of the contrasting squares. Press the seams away from the triangles. Lay out the squares in the Bowtie format and join them in pairs. Press the seams toward the darkest fabric. Assemble the pairs of squares and press the final seam open to complete the Bowties.

STEP-BY-STEP CONSTRUCTION OF BOWTIE BLOCK

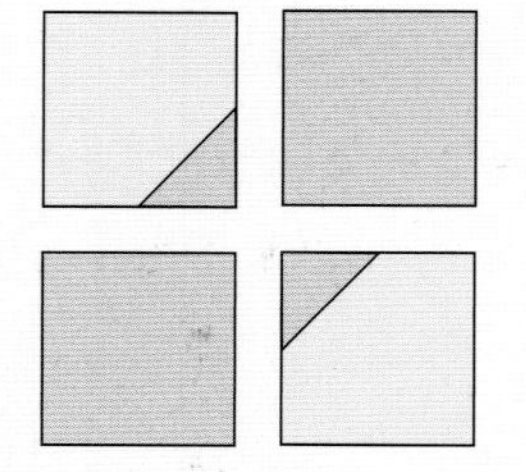

Attach corner-square triangles.

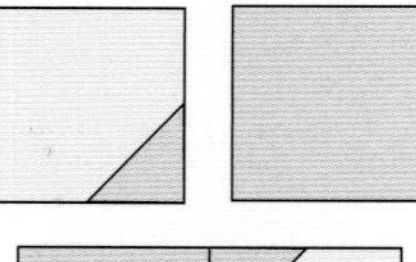

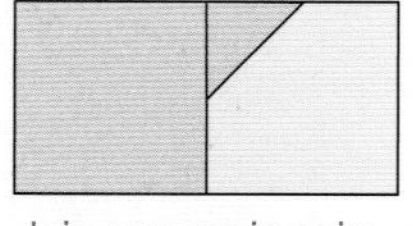

Join squares in pairs.

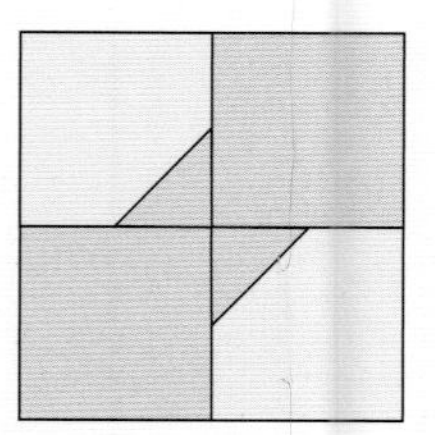

Assemble pairs to complete block.

Shoofly Blocks

Make the half-square triangles (see page 16) and trim. Assemble in rows with the other squares, pressing the seams away from the half-square triangles and the center square. Sew the rows together to complete the blocks. These directions also apply to the Monkey Wrench.

STEP-BY-STEP CONSTRUCTION OF SHOOFLY BLOCK

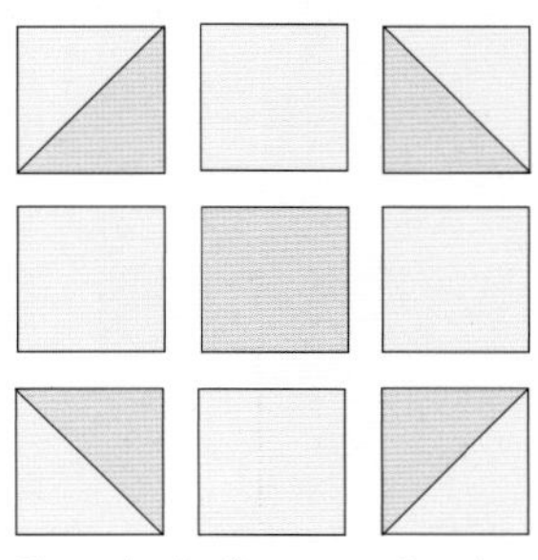

Piece the half-square triangles.

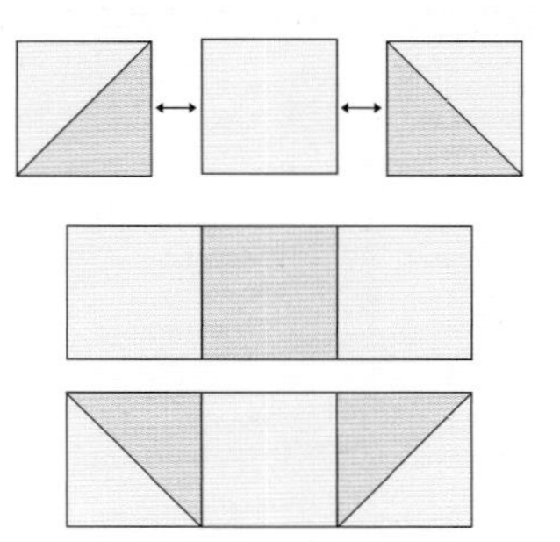

Join squares in rows.

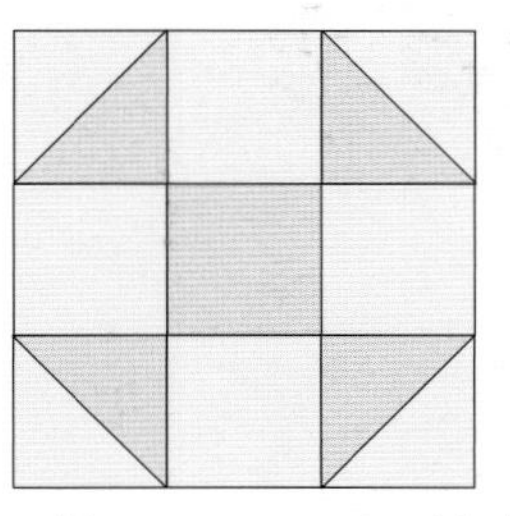

Assemble rows to complete block.

Sawtooth Star Blocks

Use the corner-square triangle method (see page15) to make the star point units from the side rectangles and the star point squares. Sew two of the units to opposite sides of the center square; press the seams toward the center square. Join the corner squares to each end of the remaining two star point units; press the seams toward the corners. Stitch the side units onto the center sections and press the seams toward the center sections.

STEP-BY-STEP CONSTRUCTION OF SAWTOOTH STAR BLOCK

Piece the star points using corner-square triangles.

Join the pieces in rows.

Assemble rows to complete block.

Ohio Star Blocks

Make the quarter-square triangle units (see page 17) and trim. Assemble in rows with the other squares, pressing the seams away from the quarter-square triangle units. Sew the rows together to complete the block.

STEP-BY-STEP CONSTRUCTION OF OHIO STAR BLOCK

Piece the quarter-square triangle units for the star points.

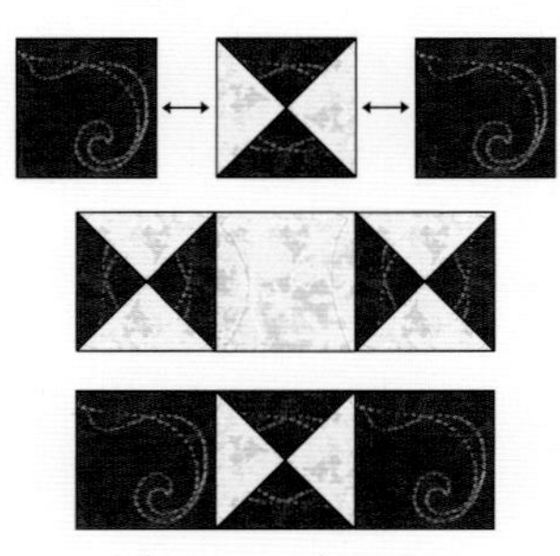

Join squares in rows.

Assemble rows to complete block.

Wedges

I have devised a template-free method to create the wedge-shaped units in the Bear's Paw Wedge block. It's similar to the corner-square triangle method, but utilizes rectangles instead of squares to create the long skinny triangles on either side of the wedge. A regular corner-square triangle (see page 15) is used next to the fat end of the wedge.

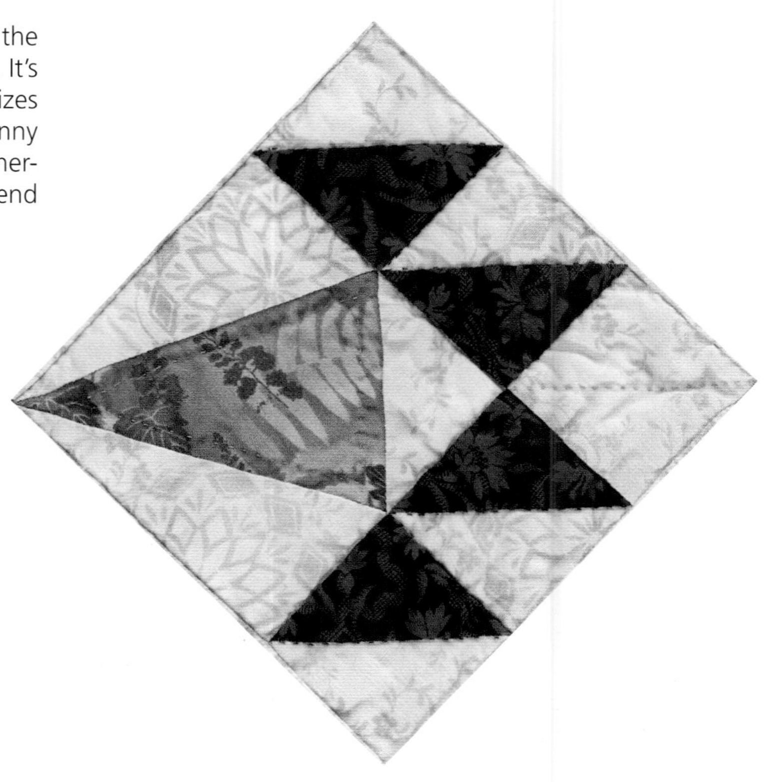

Bear's Paw Wedge

Cut squares of the wedge fabric, two rectangles for each unit for the side triangles, and one square for the corner-square triangle. Mark the backside of the rectangles as follows: a point in two diagonal corners ¼" in from the corners with a line that bisects the two points. Note that the line does not pass through the corners of the rectangles. The two rectangles should be mirror images of each other. Also mark the backside of the square with points ¼" from the edge in the places shown below. Follow the letters to help match when stitching.

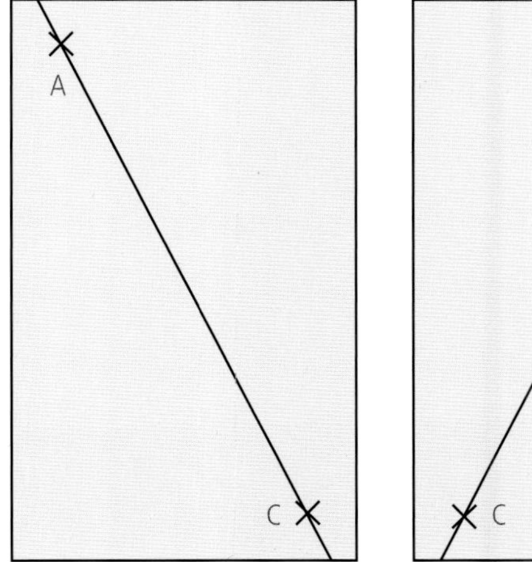

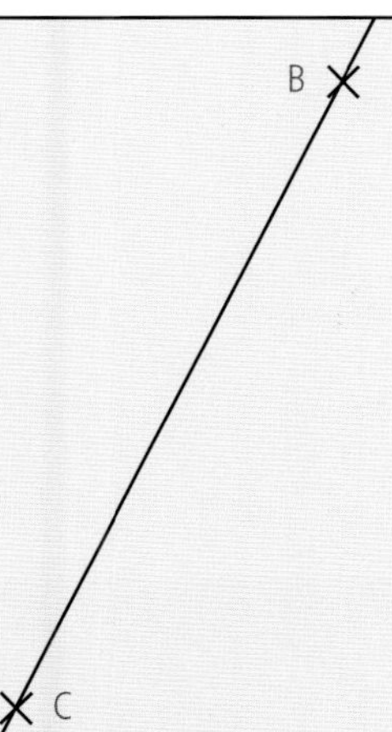

Follow letters for stitching wedges.
On wrong side of the two rectangles, mark ¼" from diagonal corners and draw lines as shown.

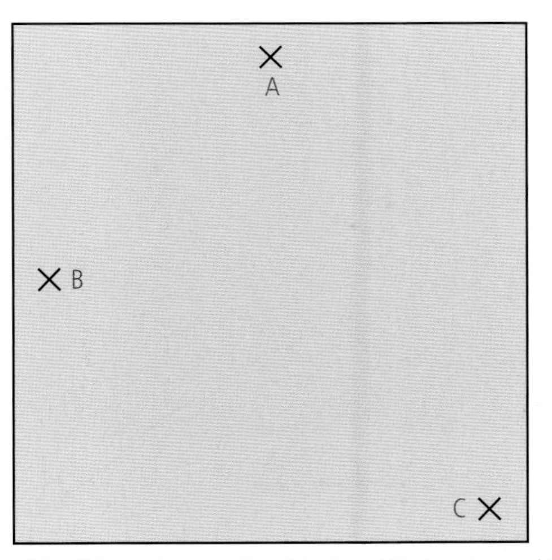

On wrong side of the square, mark points A and B at center and ¼" in from edge of fabric. Mark point C ¼" in from corner.

With right sides together, match and pin Points A and C on the first rectangle with Points A and C on the square. Poke the pins vertically through these points and shift the fabrics until they lie flat, then pin to stabilize, positioning the pins perpendicular to the line on the rectangle and stitch. Trim the excess, leaving a ¼" seam allowance. Press the seam toward the side triangle.

STEP-BY-STEP CONSTRUCTION OF WEDGES

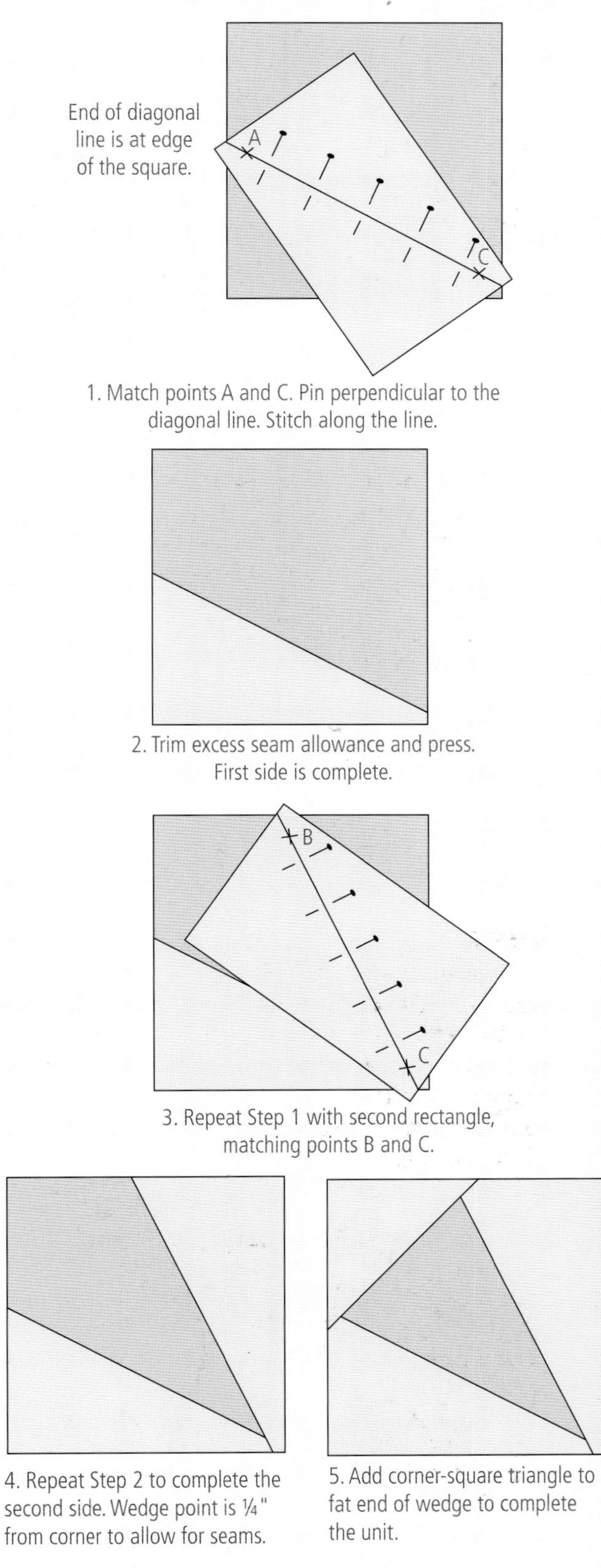

1. Match points A and C. Pin perpendicular to the diagonal line. Stitch along the line.

2. Trim excess seam allowance and press. First side is complete.

3. Repeat Step 1 with second rectangle, matching points B and C.

4. Repeat Step 2 to complete the second side. Wedge point is ¼" from corner to allow for seams.

5. Add corner-square triangle to fat end of wedge to complete the unit.

Repeat with the second rectangle, matching points B and C. To complete the unit, add the corner-square triangle at the fat end of the wedge.

Prairie Points

Prairie points are used to embellish the Ohio Star lattice quilt (see page 84) and the Monkey Wrench lattice quilt (see page 88).

Prairie points detail in Star Struck

Prairie points are easy to make and can add a delightful touch to your quilt. They are simply folded squares. Line up the raw edges between two fabrics on a seamline to piece them into the quilt top. Experiment with different sizes of squares to yield prairie points the desired size. The sample quilt features a variety of squares ranging from 2½" to 4".

FOLD FABRIC TO MAKE PRAIRIE POINTS.

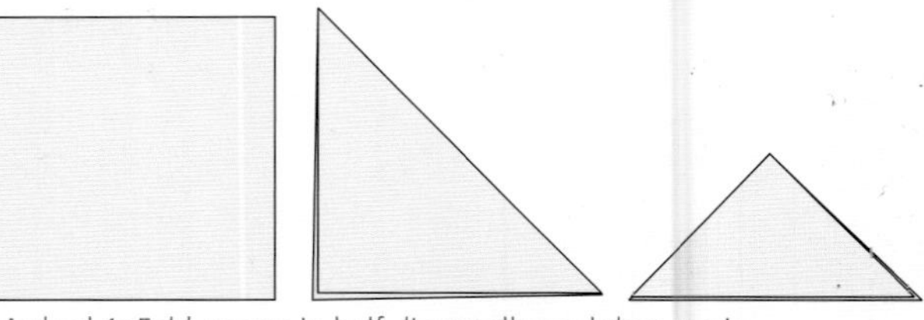

Method 1: Fold square in half diagonally, and then again.

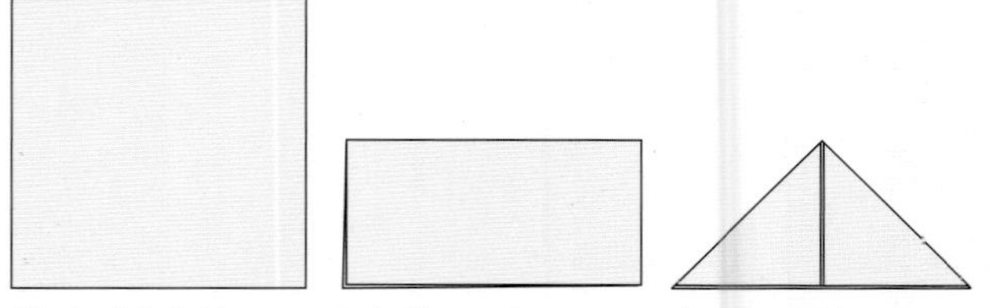

Method 2: Fold square in half to make a rectangle, then fold two corners to the center.

Piano Keys Border

A piano keys border is a wonderful way to bring all of the fabrics used in the center field of the quilt into the border and at the same time use up leftover scraps. The piano keys may be made from a variety of strip widths and positioned randomly or sequentially.

Measure the length and width of the quilt center field across the middle, (not along the edges), to obtain the required lengths of the piano keys borders. Piece the piano keys, keeping the width of the border consistent and the edges parallel. The width of the individual strips and the number of different fabrics used is entirely up to you. Manipulate the sizes of the strips at each end of the border to avoid a skinny strip next to the corner square.

Trip Around the Garden with piano keys border (See project on page 52.)

Piano keys border on Trip Around the Garden

Squares On-Point Border

Winter Garden border with large and small squares on-point. This intricate pieced border is extremely attractive, but quite challenging to execute. It's recommended only for experienced quilters.

Winter Garden, Bear's Paw variation with pieced border (see project on page 112)

The on-point pieced units are not difficult to make. The key is making them fit, because the measurement across the on-point square is not a simple fraction. When the pattern doesn't fit exactly, center the border sections and modify the corners to make a smooth symmetrical transition. If desired, put a solid or pieced square unit in the corner to avoid the need to make the pattern fit (see Southwestern Bears, page 113). Another approach is to adjust the size of the plain border strips between the center field of the quilt and the pieced border, to make the latter fit.

Begin by piecing the triangular units made of the small square and two small triangles. Fortunately, you can do this without cutting all the triangles individually. Larger units of on-point squares are constructed and cut to yield four triangle units.

STEP-BY-STEP CONSTRUCTION OF TRIANGULAR UNITS FOR PIECED BORDER.

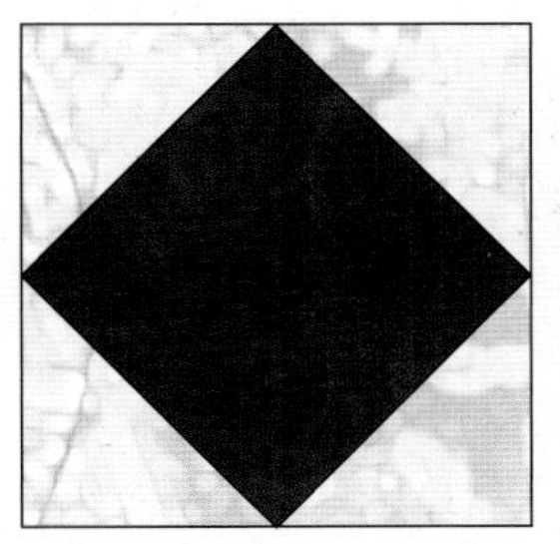

1. Sew triangles onto each side of large squares.

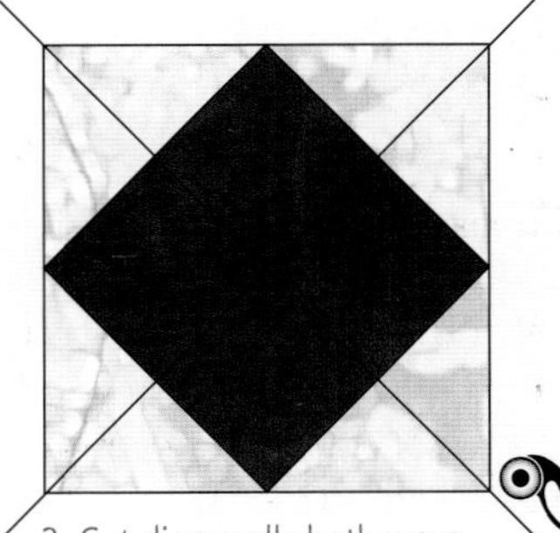

2. Cut diagonally both ways.

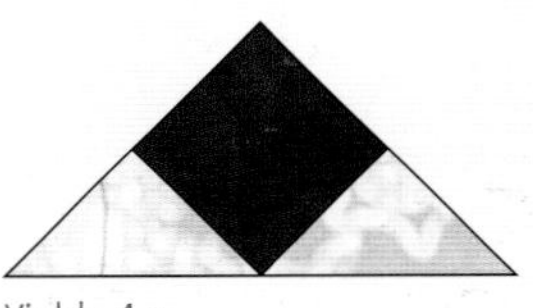

Yields 4 x

Next, join the triangular units onto the large squares in parallelograms. Assemble the parallelograms into border strips and make the four triangle units that will be placed next to the corners.

STEP-BY-STEP CONSTRUCTION OF PIECED BORDER STRIPS

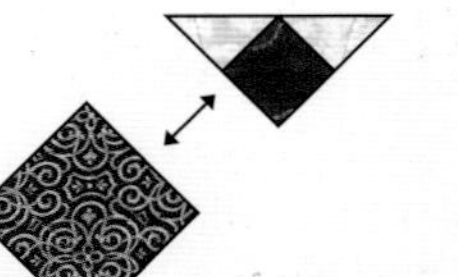

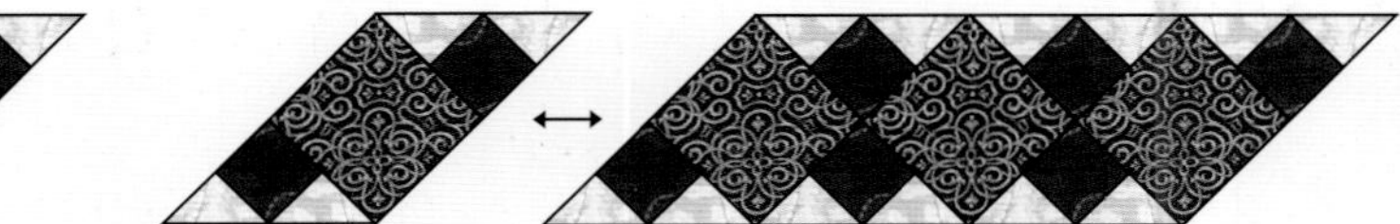

1. Join pieced triangles to large squares to make parallelograms. Place the pieced triangle on top of the square aligning the raw edges of the small and large squares. Stitch toward the small triangles.
2. Assemble the parallelograms into pieced border strips.

3. Make four triangular units - one for each strip to go adjacent to the corners.

4. Join the triangular units to complete the four border strips. For Winter Garden - 18 parallelograms and one triangular unit in each border strip.

In the corners, the small squares are adjacent, so you'll need to remove the last small triangle on each end of the border strips. You may have to remove part of another triangle seam in order to do this, and then sew it back again. Trim the border strips so that you have an exact ¼" seam allowance from the points of the large and small squares to the edge. You'll also need to make four corner sections. Each has one large square, two pieced triangle units and a plain triangle.

CORNER SECTIONS OF PIECED BORDER

1. Remove the last small triangle on each end of the border strips.

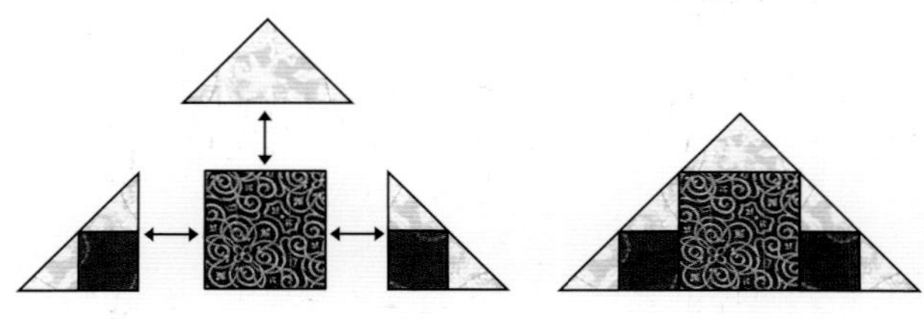

2. Make four pieced corner units. Join two pieced triangles onto large square, then add the plain triangle.

STEP-BY-STEP JOINING OF BORDER TO QUILT TOP

1. Attach narrow inner border strips to the pieced border. Trim ends as shown.

Trim border strip at 45-degree angle, in line with the edge of red square.

Join the plain inside border strips to the pieced borders and attach to the center field of the quilt top. Miter the corners of both borders at once (see page 28). Alternatively, add the inside border strips first without mitering. Add the corner sections.

2. Attach to quilt top, mitering the corners.
3. Join pieced corner-triangle sections.

Assembling and Completing the Quilt

Assembling Blocks and Adding Borders

The way that your quilt top is assembled will dramatically affect the appearance. Good fabric choices to frame or sash the blocks and add outer borders will greatly enhance the look of the quilt. Here are some setting options:

Blocks set square and adjacent

Blocks with sashing strips in between; cornerstones at intersections optional

Blocks with pieced sashing strips; cornerstones at intersections optional

Frame each block and then add sashing strips; cornerstones at intersections optional

Blocks on-point

Medallion-style

Blocks in an irregular setting

Your quilt should be constructed so that the block outer edges, sashing strips, and borders are on the fabric straight-of-grain (lengthwise or crosswise). This includes setting triangles at the sides of quilts with blocks set on-point. Bias edges stretch and become distorted easily causing inaccuracies and waviness. This effect can easily become more pronounced with each border that is added unless care is taken to make precise measurements. Sometimes bias edges are unavoidable, in which case you should handle them as little as possible and sew them in at the earliest opportunity.

When adding sashing strips to blocks, always press the seam allowances away from the blocks and toward the sashing strips. The same applies for frames and outer borders. If you add cornerstones to the sashing intersections, press the seam allowances toward the sashing. Then, when all the pieces are joined, the seam allowances will abut in opposing directions and the seams will lie smoothly at the intersections.

Always stitch in an order that allows you to sew in straight lines without insetting any seams. Assemble the blocks in rows with their sashing strips, then join the rows together with the sashing that separates the rows. It's helpful to number the patchwork pieces with small sticky labels to keep them in the correct order when sewing. Avoid ironing over the labels as the heat may make the glue extra sticky and leave a residue on the fabric.

BLOCK SETTINGS

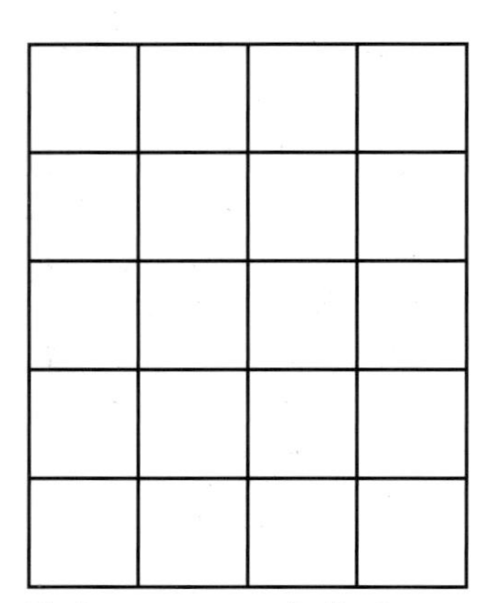

Blocks set square and adjacent

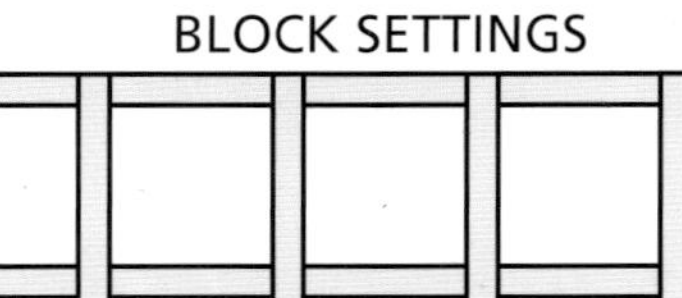

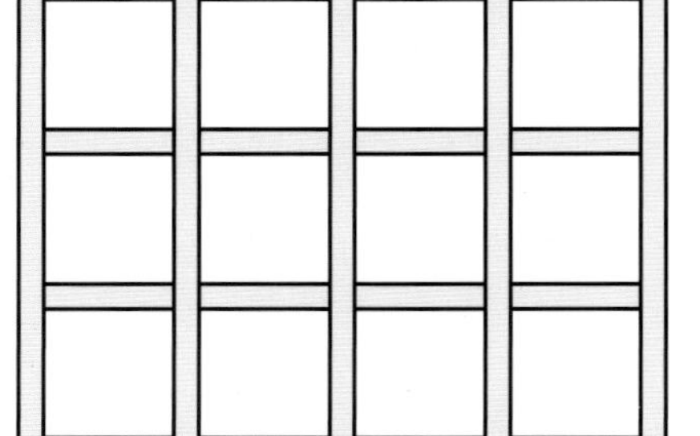

Blocks set square with sashing strips

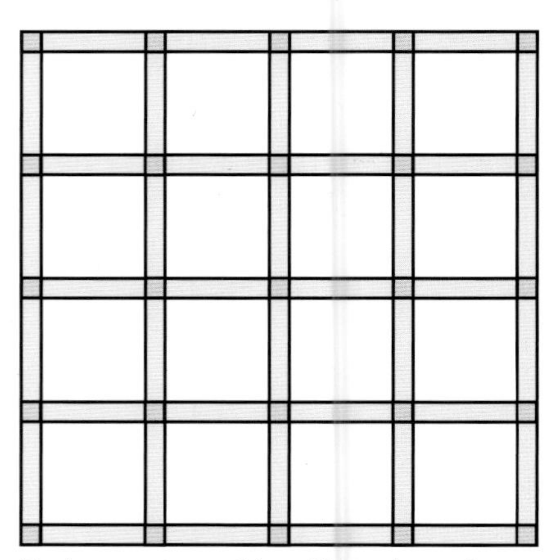

Blocks set square with sashing strips and cornerstones at intersections

Blocks set on-point and adjacent

Blocks set on-point with sashing strips

Blocks set on-point with sashing strips and cornerstones at intersections

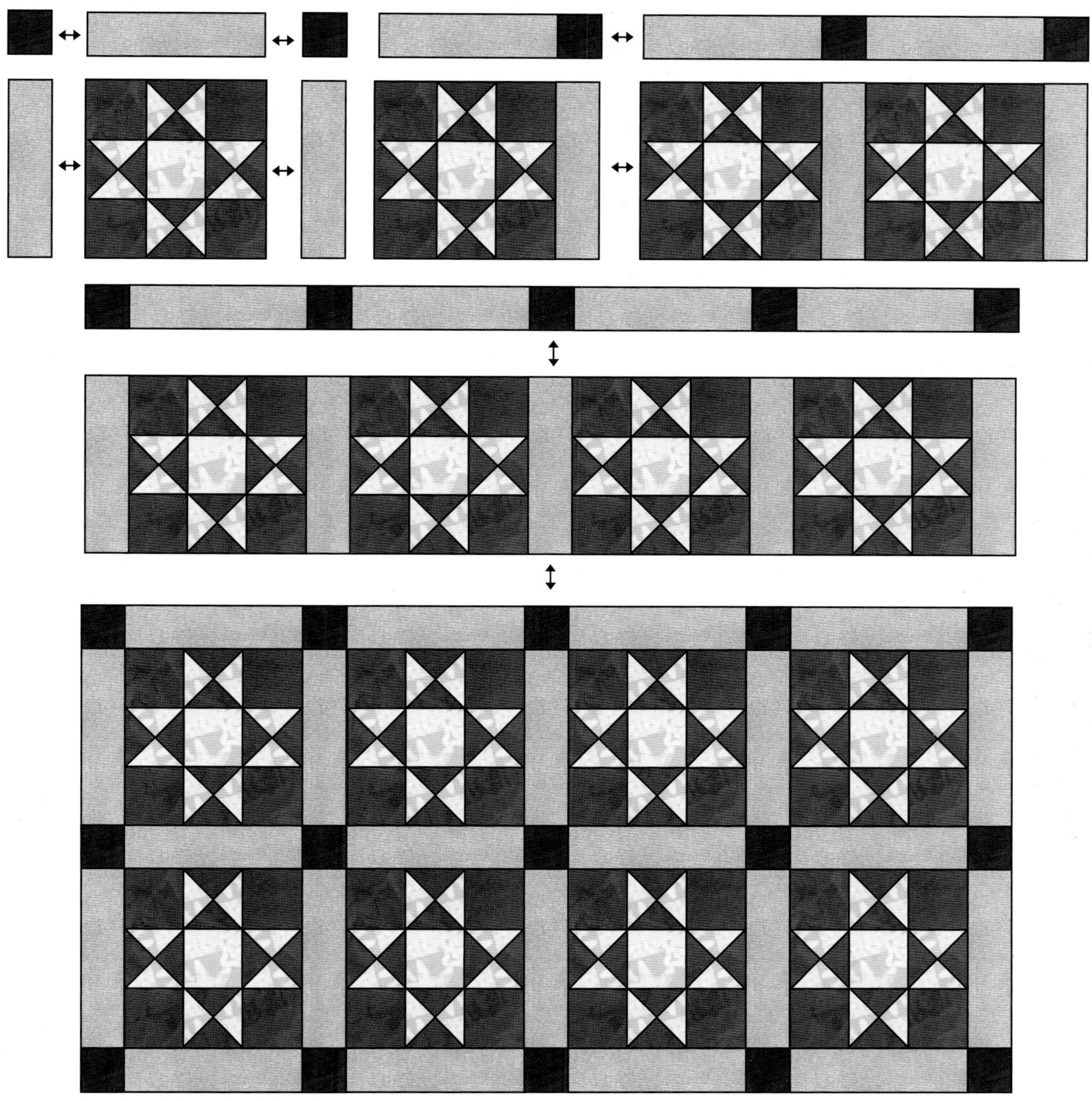

Assemble blocks with sashing strips and cornerstones.
Join sashing strips to cornerstones in rows. Join blocks to sashing strips in rows. Assemble the rows.

For blocks set on-point, rows will be on the diagonal and have setting triangles on the outer edges. When sewing the setting triangles to the blocks, align the square corners so that the excess on the triangles is at the 45-degree end. Trim the extra triangles from the seam allowances after stitching. The corner triangles should be centered on the blocks so that there are excess triangles at each end. If the setting triangles and corners were originally cut larger than needed, the edges of the center field may be irregular. Trim for an accurate ¼" seam allowance all the way around.

ASSEMBLE ON-POINT BLOCKS WITH SETTING TRIANGLES AND TRIM.

Adjacent blocks
Join in diagonal rows.
Assemble rows.

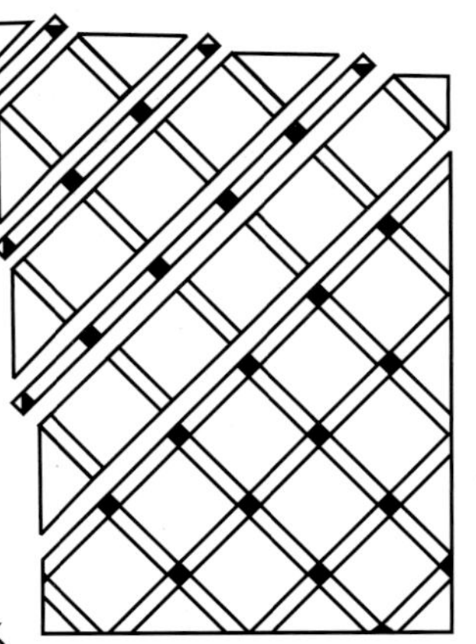
Blocks with sashing strips and cornerstones
Join in diagonal rows.
Assemble rows.

Irregular edges on the center field

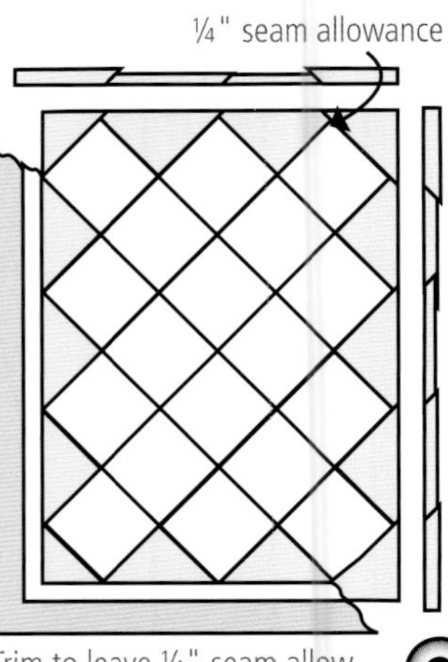

Trim to leave ¼" seam allowance. Borders will come to the corners of the blocks.

For frames and borders: first attach two opposite sides, then join the remaining two sides. When adding borders to a quilt top, measure the distance across the center and not the edge of the patchwork (which tends to distort), and use this to calculate the size of the strips to cut for the border. If you simply cut the border strip the same size as a stretched edge, the quilt will become even more misshapen and it will not hang squarely. The edge may be a little longer or shorter than the center, necessitating easing in of the extra border or center field, and distributing it evenly along the entire seam length. (See page 14 for instructions on pinning.) Double-check your measurements if the discrepancy is large.

If a border is longer than the full width of the fabric (42"), cut it lengthwise from the fabric or piece it. Piece with a 45-degree angle seam, matching the fabric as accurately as possible. This is much less visible than a seam straight across the strip. Take the time to tackle this stage with care and precision, even when you may be eager to finish the project.

Mitered Corners

Mitered corners will add a professional looking touch to your quilt, especially on quilts that have multiple border strips. For multiple borders, first join the border strips together, so when attached to the quilt, you can miter all of them at once.

Mitered corner on Basket of Fuchsias (see project on page 48)

1 Measure the quilt across the middle (not along the sides) in both directions. Cut the borders this length, plus two times their width and about 3" extra to allow plenty of fabric to accommodate the corners. For example, finished quilt center = 41" x 51", finished border width = 3", cut the borders: 2 @ 41 + (2 x 3) + 3 = 50" and 2 @ 51 + (2 x 3) + 3 = 60".

2 Center the border strips. Using a pencil or pin, measure and mark the dimension of the quilt side minus ¼" at each end.

3 Pin two opposite borders before sewing. Position the mark at each end ¼" from the top corners. If the sides of the quilt are distorted, the border strip may not be exactly the same size. In this case, ease in any excess evenly and make it fit (see above).

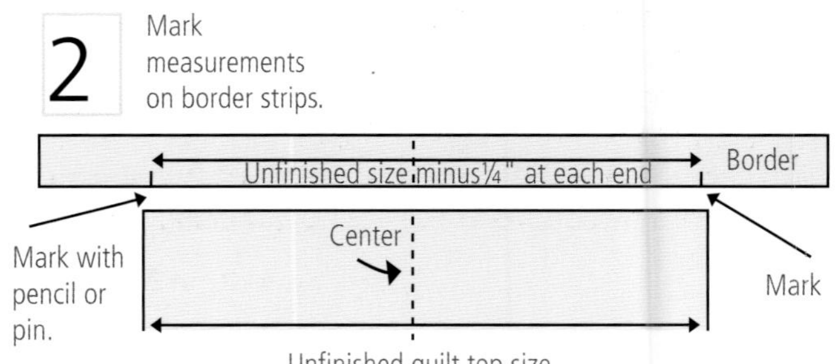

4 Start sewing ½" to 1" away from the mark, first backstitching to the mark but not beyond it. Stitch along the length of the side until you reach the mark at the other end, but not beyond it; backstitch three or four stitches. Attach the opposite side in the same way. Press the seam allowances toward the border strips.

5 Pin and sew the remaining two sides. When you reach the corners, be careful not to stitch onto the two already attached border strips. Press the seam allowances as above.

6 Use a pencil to mark the miters at each corner on the wrong side of each border section. Using a 6" x 24" mitering ruler, find the 45-degree angle on the ruler and line this up with the seamline. The edge of the ruler should be in the corner exactly where the stitching line ends. Alternatively, use a mitering ruler. Make sure that the border section is flat and straight before marking.

7 Carefully pin the corners matching the marked lines on the two pieces. Extra care will be needed when the border contains multiple strips, because these must match exactly when joined. Backstitch three or four stitches into the corner where the border joins the quilt, but not beyond it; stitch to the outer edge. Check that the seam is accurate before cutting away the excess fabric. Press the seam allowance to one side or open.

MARK MITERED CORNER FOR STITCHING.

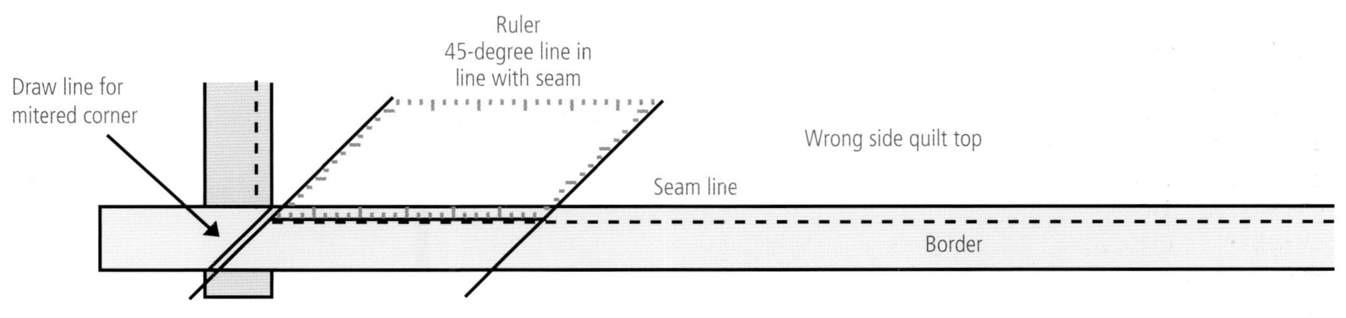

Quilt Backing

Quilt backs for small quilts are easy to make. Cut the back a little larger (at least 1½" on each side) than the quilt top. Allow this extra amount on all quilt backs in case of fabric uptake or distortion during quilting. The excess quilt backing and batting is trimmed after the binding is attached by machine and before the binding is stitched by hand.

For quilts larger than 42" wide, the quilt back must be pieced, unless wider fabric is purchased. Many quilting stores have a small selection of wide fabrics that make excellent quilt backs. This is an economical way to buy the fabric and avoids the necessity for seams. Use the fabric efficiently by planning carefully. Long cuts of fabric are needed for border strips on the quilt top, but the leftovers may be used to piece the quilt back, so that you don't necessarily have to buy two or more full quilt lengths of 42"-wide backing fabric. For example, the backside of Quick Tripper was pieced from the leftovers of two yard pieces in a strippy design, making the quilt reversible.

Quick Tripper reversible quilt, topside and backside (81" x 81")

Batting and Basting

There are many types of batting available. Read the package carefully for content information, including the height of the loft, and how far apart you can stitch the lines of quilting. 100-percent cotton is warm, but usually requires a higher density of quilting than polyester batting. 80-percent cotton and 20-percent polyester is often a good compromise, because the polyester bonds the cotton, so quilting lines may be further apart. Some cotton battings contain a scrim, which is a very thin mesh of plastic to hold the cotton together. These work well for wall hangings. I like to use low or medium loft, but if you want a poofy look, choose the high loft. Polyester tends to be poofier than cotton. Wool and silk battings also are available, but they are more expensive. Some types of batting shrink when washed. Check the directions on the package to see if it's necessary to launder the batting before use.

Basting stitches hold the three layers of the quilt together until the quilting step is completed, then the stitches are removed. Secure the layers with long basting stitches in a grid pattern; with safety pins; or by using a basting gun with plastic tacks. Spray adhesives or iron-on batting are also options. (My preference is to use traditional basting stitches.)

1 Press the quilt top and the quilt back (the seams on the quilt back may be pressed open).

2 Lay the quilt back flat, wrong side up, on a table (with a non-scratch surface or one that you don't mind scratching), hard floor, or low-pile carpet. (I use a table for small quilts and baste large quilts on the floor.)

3 Tape the quilt back to the surface with masking tape or use T-pins on a carpet. Secure the opposing sides, working from the center out to the corners. Repeat for the remaining two sides. Make sure the quilt back is perfectly flat. It should be taut but not stretched to distortion.

4 Place the batting on top of the backing. Gently smooth it so that there are no wrinkles.

5 Place the quilt top, right-side up, over the batting. Make sure it's positioned centrally over the quilt back and that there is a margin of quilt back and batting exposed around each edge (at least 1½"). Check that it's perfectly flat and square. Straight seams sometimes appear a little crooked and the quilt top may be gently manipulated to align them correctly.

6 When working on a carpet, T-pin the quilt top as you did the back. On a table, put safety pins in the corners and the center of each side through all three layers.

Use a spoon to baste.
Photo by Mark Frey

7 Use quilting or regular thread, a large needle and a spoon to lift the needle from the surface. Baste a grid of long running stitches over the quilt. Start in the middle of one side of the quilt and baste all the way across. You may knot the thread or make a couple of backstitches to start. Take four or five stitches before pulling the thread all the way through. This saves time, especially if your thread is long. The second line of basting stitches should be about a hand's width away from the first. Continue basting the lines until you are near the edges. Then baste at right angles, creating a grid.

8 Remove the tape or pins from the edges and baste all the way around the quilt ½" to 1" from the edges.

9 Quilt; then remove the basting stitches except for those around the quilt perimeter. Remove these after the binding is attached.

Quilting

The quilting stitches are a vital component because they hold the three layers of the quilt sandwich together. They may also greatly enhance the appearance of the quilt. Quilting stitch patterns show up particularly well on solid colors, as well as light monochromatic fabrics and small prints. The quilting stitches may be sewn by machine — commercially or on a home machine — or by hand, and should be an even density. Quilting lines may follow or echo the geometric piecing pattern, or be completely different. As with piecing, there are numerous options. Details are provided on the quilting designs for each featured project. Refer to other books for instructions on the techniques of hand and machine quilting.

Hand quilting is relaxing and rewarding, if you have the time, and it gives the quilt a wonderful soft texture. One of the featured quilts, Pacific Northwest Bears (see page 102) is hand quilted.

Pacific Northwest Bears detail illustrates hand quilting.

When machine quilting, I suggest stabilizing the quilt by quilting in the ditch along the seams between the blocks before quilting inside the blocks. Quilting accurately in the ditch may be challenging, so alternatively, use a serpentine stitch along the seams, or in a diagonal grid. This is a very forgiving technique and looks especially attractive in variegated rayon threads. Change the machine needle to a size 90 topstitching needle when using specialty threads. Use a walking foot for straight line stitching. Drop the feed-dogs and use a darning foot for free-motion quilting.

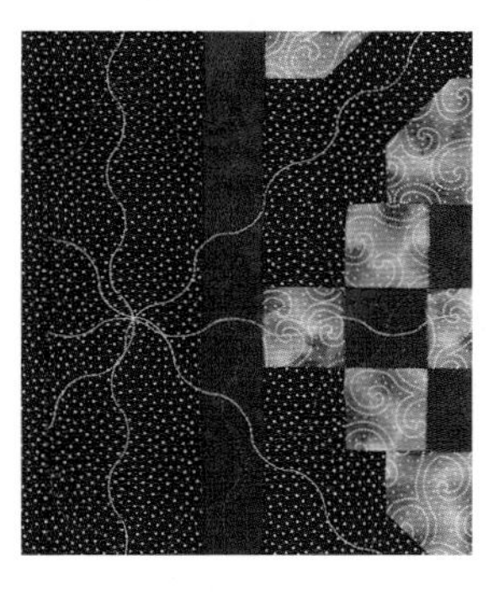

Date Night Tripper illustrates machine quilting with a grid of serpentine stitches.

Consider sending large quilts (over about 60" square) to an outside source for machine quilting on a long-arm machine, if you don't have time or don't want to handle the bulk of a large quilt. Commercial quilters offer a wide range of pattern options, from all over pantographs to custom designs. Discuss the possibilities with your quilter.

Binding

Binding strips may be cut on the straight-of-grain unless the quilt has curved or irregular edges. I recommend a French (double) binding because it's strong and durable and finishes the quilt with a firm edge.

1 Calculate the number of binding strips needed by measuring the perimeter of the quilt and dividing by 40 for fabric 42" wide.

2 Cut 2½"-wide binding strips. For flannel, 3" strips are recommended.

3 Cut the ends of the strips at 45-degrees and join them together.

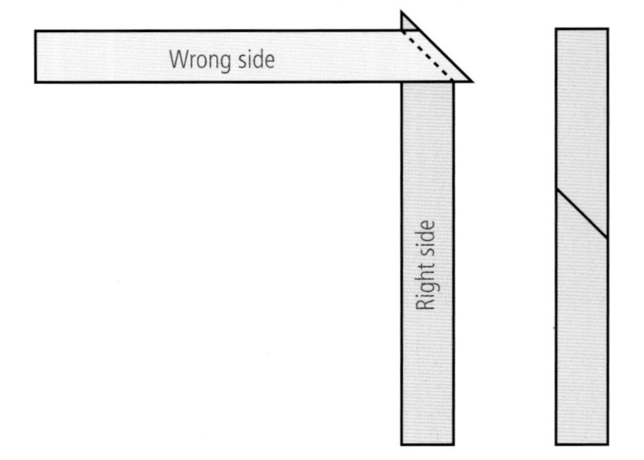

4 Press the seams open and press the binding in half lengthwise with the wrong sides together.

5 The project should be quilted, but still have basting stitches ½" to 1" from the outer edge. Align the raw edge of the binding with the raw edge of the quilt top. Start stitching about 10" below a corner, leaving a tail of 6" to 8" of binding for joining at the end. Use a walking foot, if available. Stop ¼" from the first corner, make three or four backstitches, and remove the quilt from the sewing machine.

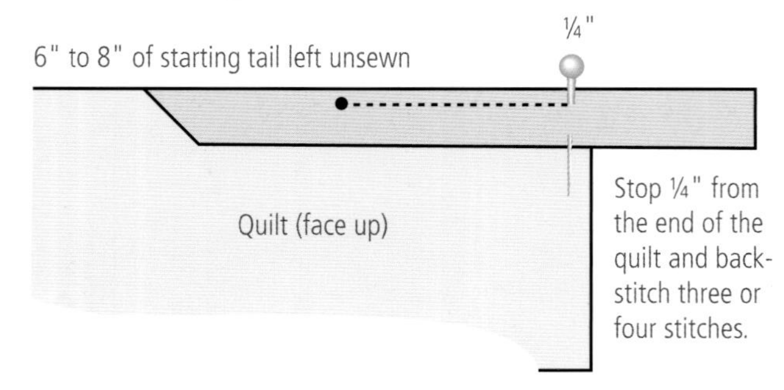

6 Rotate the quilt a quarter turn and fold the binding straight up, away from the corner, making a 45-degree angle fold. Bring the binding straight down in line with the next raw edge to be sewn. The top fold of the binding should be even with the edge just sewn.

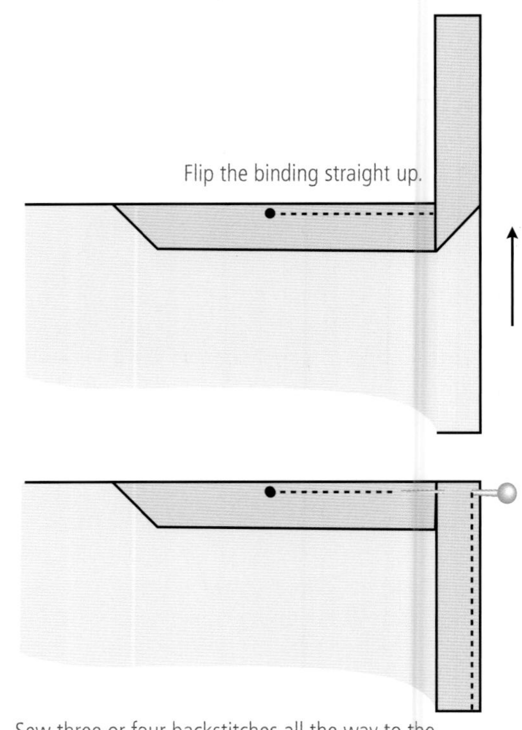

Sew three or four backstitches all the way to the edge, then proceed forward to the next corner.

7 Start stitching with backstitches right to the edge of the top fold, then stitch until you reach ¼" from the next corner. Stop and backstitch. Continue on all sides of the quilt.

8 Fold the binding at the corner as previously described and pin it by the top fold.

9 Trim the end of the binding in a 45-degree angle. Open the binding ends and draw a pencil line at 45-degrees where they join. Cut the tail ½" away from the line to accommodate the seam allowance. Sew the binding ends together and finger-press the seam open.

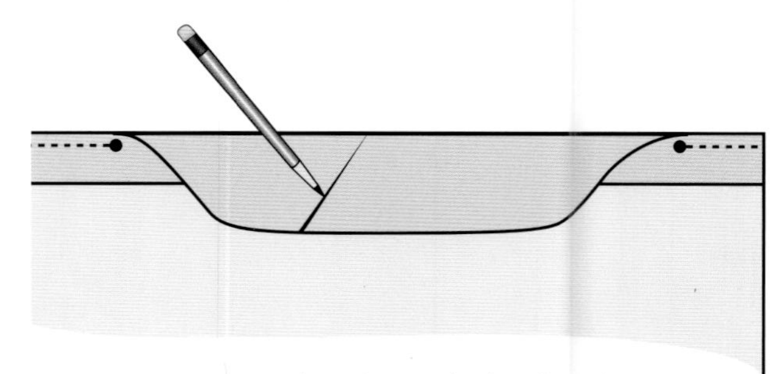

Cut two tails so they overlap by 2" to 3".

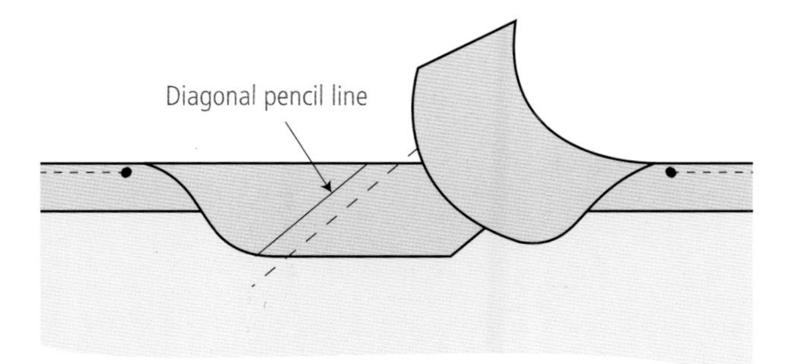

Cut the ending tail ½" longer than the diagonal pencil line.

10 Sew the binding down, beginning with the backstitches at the corner and continue until reaching the starting point.

11 Remove the basting stitches.

12 Use a rotary cutter or scissors to trim the excess batting and backing flush with the quilt top and binding raw edge. The binding should be stuffed evenly with batting, so trim carefully.

13 Bring the folded edge of the binding to the back of the quilt so that it covers the machine stitching line. Hand stitch it down with a blind stitch using thread that matches the binding rather than the quilt back.

14 Miter the corners by folding the unstitched binding from the next side over to form the 45-degree angle. Another way to bind is to machine sew the binding to the back of the quilt, then wrap it to the front and topstitch with a zigzag or decorative machine stitch as in Ditsy Garden (quilt pattern on page 36).

The Finishing Touches

To add embellishments to your quilt use buttons, beads, embroidery, or anything you like to give it more pizzazz. Add a label to the backside. Years from now, people will be curious about who made the quilt, when, and where. (I usually position the label in a lower corner of the quilt where it's easy to see by lifting the corner when the quilt is hanging.)

To hang the quilt, attach a sleeve to the back along the top edge. The sleeve is a fabric tube wide enough to accommodate a dowel, which may be hung on hooks or suspended by fishing line from museum-style hangers on the wall.

1930s Trip Around the World from the collection of Joe and Mary Koval

CHAPTER THREE

Trip Around the World

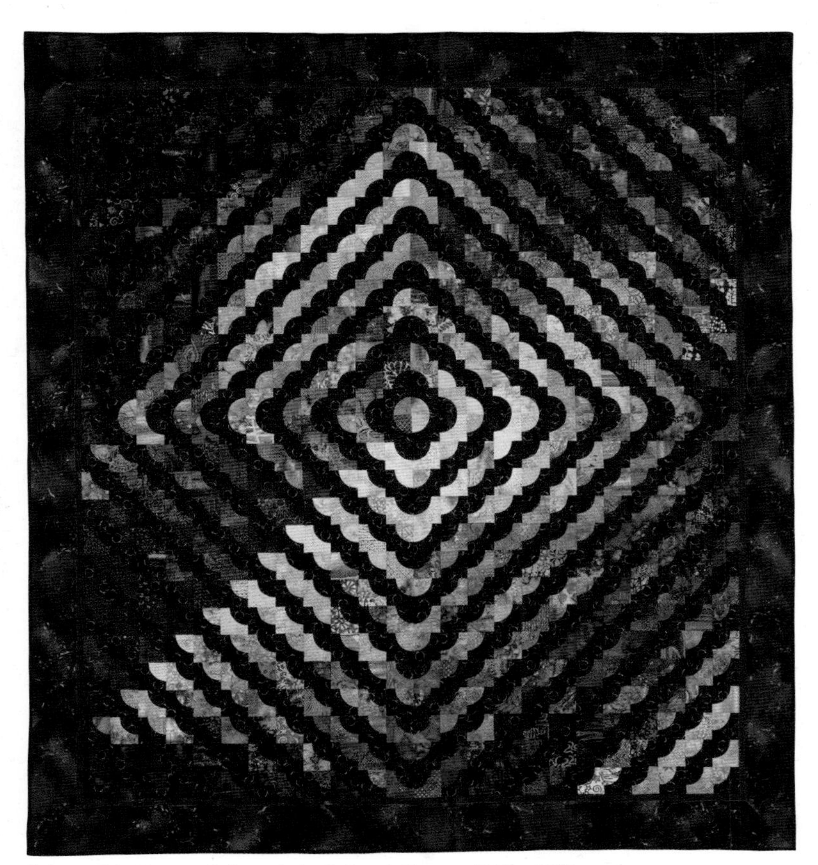

If the Amish Went to Bali made by Deborah Haynes (86" x 82")
Photo by Mark Frey

The traditional Trip Around the World pattern consists of many small squares with the colors arranged in concentric rows on-point around the center. Play with this format — as shown in the sample projects — enlarging the squares, substituting the squares for pieced blocks and inserting sashing. Here is an example.

If the Amish Went to Bali has Drunkard's Path units instead of squares, but the Trip Around the World configuration is immediately apparent. Deborah hand pieced all the small Drunkard's Path units, assembled them by machine and finished with machine quilting. The dark background on alternating rows provides a rich setting for the gorgeous array of colorful batik fabrics that make this quilt glow.

Ditsy Garden

SKILL LEVEL: EASY This bright and cheerful lap quilt, combining large squares and four-patches, is an ideal beginner project. The sample features fleece on the back and there is no batting. This simplifies the construction and makes it a perfect project to share with smaller helping hands. Kids love the soft fleece backing and will be eager to participate and learn.

MATERIALS AND CUTTING FOR DITSY GARDEN

Quilt size: 58½" x 58½"   Block size: 6½"

Materials	Yards	Cutting
Light blue (squares, four-patches)	½	(4) 7" squares
		(2) full-width 3¾" strips
Mono purple (squares, four-patches)	½	(5) 7" squares
		(2) full-width 3¾" strips
Mono purple (binding)	½	(6) full-width 2½" strips
Light pink (squares, four-patches)	¾	(8) 7" squares
		(2) full-width 3¾" strips
Mono magenta (squares, four-patches)	¾	(8) 7" squares
		(2) full-width 3¾" strips
Yellow/multi dragonflies (squares)	¼	(4) 7" squares
Purple/multi large flowers (squares)	½	(8) 7" squares
Purple/multi small flowers (squares)	1	(16) 7" squares
Multi flowers/dragonfly (squares)	¾	(12) 7" squares
Fleece 60" wide (backing)	1¾	

Constructing Ditsy Garden

1 Strip-piece the light blue and mono purple 3¾" strips (see page 15). Press the seam allowances toward the dark and counter-cut (16) 3¾". Use these to make eight four-patch blocks.

2 Repeat for the light pink and mono magenta strips.

3 Lay out all the squares and four-patches in the desired configuration. Use the photograph as a guide or rearrange them into your own pattern.

4 Join together in rows and press the seam allowances so that adjacent rows are in opposing directions.

5 Assemble the rows.

6 Lay the quilt back flat, wrong side up, on a firm surface. Place the quilt top, right-side up, over the backing. (No batting was used on the sample quilt.) Baste and quilt as desired. The top clings nicely to the fleece, so the quilting stitches may be relatively far apart. The sample quilt features a diagonal grid of serpentine stitches.

7 Attach the binding. On the sample quilt, the binding was sewn onto the back side, then wrapped to the front, and sewed in place using variegated rayon thread and a small zigzag stitch.

Quick Tripper

Quick Tripper pieced by the author, machine quilted by Wanda Rains (81" x 81")

SKILL LEVEL: EASY Quick Tripper is fast and easy to make. This warm and colorful flannel quilt is big enough for a bed, or a vibrant accessory for a den or kid's playroom. Note how the coloring of the sashing strips inserted between the squares augments the Trip Around the World pattern. Feel free to improvise in your own way. I made a strippy pattern on the back, to make the quilt reversible.

MATERIALS AND CUTTING FOR QUICK TRIPPER

Quilt size: 81" x 81" Block size: 7"

Note: Begin with 2 yards of each fabric and use leftovers from quilt top to piece quilt back, if desired.

Materials	Yards	Cutting
Purple particles	¼	(5) 7½" squares
Yellow/blue stripes	¼	(4) 7½" squares
Pink waves	¾	(12) 7½" squares
Magenta swirls	¾	(12) 7½" squares
Purple stars	¾	(12) 7½" squares
Green particles	½	(8) 7½" squares
Green (sashing)	¾	(56) 7½" x 2¾" cut from (4) full-width 7½" strips
Yellow (sashing)	¾	(56) 7½" x 2¾" cut from (4) full-width 7½" strips
Purple (cornerstones)	½	(64) 2¾" squares cut from (5) full-width 2¾" strips
Purple/green strips (border)	2	(4) 7½" x 67½"
Binding	1	(9) full-width 3" strips (Optional: use variety of fabrics)
Batting 84" x 84"		
Backing 84" x 84"		Optional: pieced backing

Constructing Quick Tripper

1 Lay out all the squares with sashing strips and cornerstones in the desired configuration. Use the photograph as a guide or rearrange them into your own pattern.

2 Join the pieces in rows, pressing all seam allowances toward the sashing strips. Assemble the rows (see page 25).

3 Add border strips to the right and left sides. Join the pink corner squares onto the ends of the two remaining border strips; attach them to the quilt top and bottom.

4 Piece the backing, if desired. The sample quilt features 10 different flannel fabrics on the backside; cut two full width 10" strips, plus two or three extras. Each long strip has at least three different fabrics of varying lengths. The diagonal seamlines make the design livelier, especially when oriented in different directions.

5 Lay the quilt back flat, wrong side up, on a firm surface. Place the batting on top of the backing and smooth out. Layer the quilt top, right-side up, over the backing. Baste the layers and quilt as desired. The sample was quilted with a wavy pattern across the top. The curves soften the look of the quilt, adding a pleasing texture to the surface. The quilting pattern works well on both sides of the reversible quilt.

6 Bind the quilt. (3"-wide strips are recommended for flannel.) The sample quilt features leftover pieces from a variety of fabrics in the binding, bringing all the colors out to the edge.

Mini Trippers

SKILL LEVEL: AVERAGE Mini Trippers are attractive as wall hangings, or the perfect size for doll quilts. Spring Stars and Date Night Tripper are made from 3" blocks. In both quilts, I use the colors in the nine-patch blocks to accentuate the Trip Around the World format. Spring Stars is made entirely of Sawtooth Stars and nine-patches. Date Night Tripper also utilizes Bowties and four-patches.

Spring Stars

Spring Stars made by author (19½" x 19½")

There are 25 blocks, eight of which are Sawtooth Stars and all the rest are nine-patches. In my first attempt at this little quilt, I made the corner stars with the purple fabric and was disappointed to find that the purple and blue just merged together to look like one large square. Using odd scraps of pink, I cut out little triangles and placed them over the purple. The difference was astonishing, and the pink stars popped out like little gems. Ripping out the stitches was in order. Out came the purple stars and in went new pink stars for the corners. This illustrates the importance of value in creating a pleasing design.

MATERIALS AND CUTTING FOR SPRING STARS

Quilt size: 19½" x 19½"   Block size: 3"

Materials	Yards	Cutting
Blue (blocks)	¼	Stars – From (1) full-width 2" and (2) full-width 1¼" strips: Corner squares (32) 1¼" squares Side rectangles (32) 1¼" x 2" Center squares (8) 2" squares
Blue (binding)	¼	(2) full-width 2½" strips
Pink (blocks)	¼	Star points – (64) 1¼" squares from (2) full-width strips
		Nine-patches – (2) full-width 1½" strips
Light floral (blocks)	¼	Nine-patches – (4) full-width 1½" strips
Light green (blocks, borders)	¼	Nine-patches – (1) full-width 1½" strip
		Borders – (2) 1" x 15½", (2) 1" x 16½"
Purple (blocks, borders)	¼	Nine-patches – (2) full-width 1½" strips
		Borders – (2) 2" x 16½", (2) 2" x 19½"
Batting 23" x 23"		

Constructing Spring Stars

1 Construct the eight Sawtooth Star blocks (see page 19).

2 Construct the 17 nine-patch blocks (see page 15). Before sewing, cut the full-width 1½" strips into smaller sections according to the number of three-square units needed, plus a couple of inches to allow for errors: 26" for 16 units, 23" for 14 units, 14" for eight units, 10" for four units, and 3" for one unit. Strip-piece the 1½" strips. Press the seams toward the purple and pink strips, and then counter-cut them 1½" to create the three-square units. Join these units to complete the nine-patches.

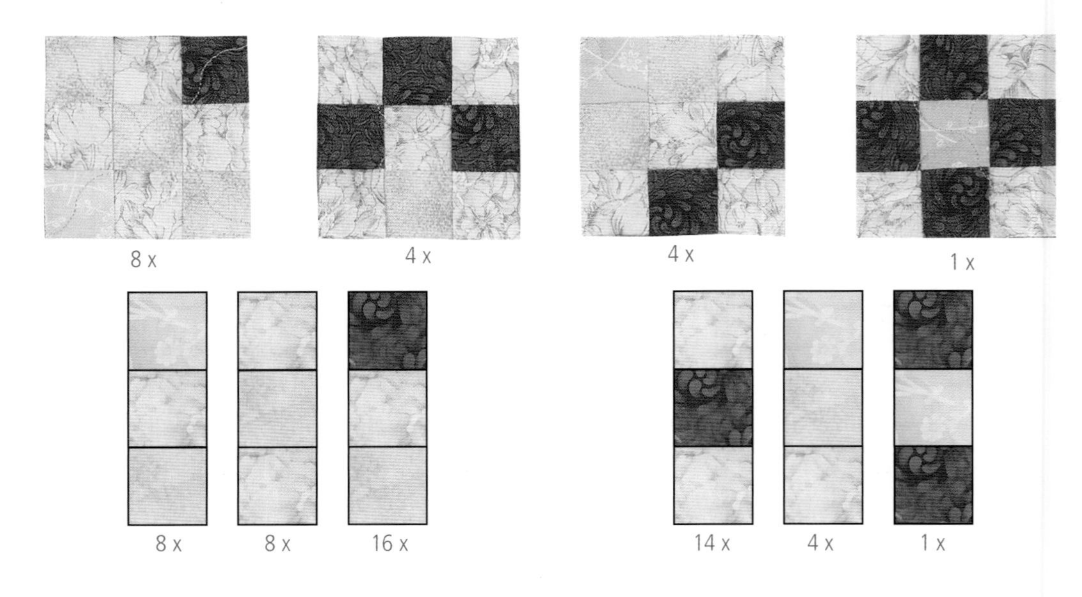

Nine-patches in Spring Stars and the three-square units required to make them

3 Lay out the 25 blocks in order and piece them in rows. Press the seams so that adjacent rows abut in opposing directions. Assemble the rows (see page 25).

4 Sew the 15½" inner borders to the left and right sides, then the 16½" borders to the top and bottom. Repeat to sew the 16½" outer borders to the sides and the 19½" borders to the top and bottom. Alternatively, miter the border corners (see page 28).

5 Lay the quilt back flat, wrong side up, on a firm surface. Place the batting on top of the backing and smooth out. Layer the quilt top, right-side up, over the backing. Baste the layers and quilt as desired. The sample quilt features a diagonal grid of serpentine stitches.

6 Bind the quilt.

Date Night Tripper

Date Night Tripper made by the author (27" x 27")

This little quilt has 49 blocks – nine Sawtooth Stars, 16 Bowties, eight four-patches and 16 nine-patches. You can easily change the pattern by rotating the Bowties and four-patches. Feel free to experiment to create your own pleasing block arrangement.

MATERIALS AND CUTTING FOR DATE NIGHT TRIPPER

Quilt size: 19½" x 19½" Block size: 3"

Materials	Yards	Cutting
Yellow (blocks)	¼	Star points - (72) 1¼" squares from (3) full-width strips
		Star centers – (9) 2" squares
Blue (blocks)	½	Stars - from (3) full-width 1¼" strips
		Side rectangles – (36) 1¼" x 2"
		Corner squares – (36) 1¼" squares
		Nine-patches - (3) full-width 1½" strips
		Bowties - (32) 2" squares from (2) full-width strips
		Four-patches – (1) full-width 2" strip
Red (blocks, border)	⅓	Nine-patches – (2) full-width 1½" strips
		Four-patches – (1) 2" x 20" strip
		Borders – (2) 1¼" x 21½", (2) 1¼" x 23"
Black (blocks, border)	¾	Nine-patches – (2) full-width 1½" strips
		Bowties – (32) 2" squares from (2) full-width strips
		Corner triangles - (32) 1¼" squares from (1) full-width strip
		Four-patches – (1) 2" x 20" strip
		Borders (2) 2½" x 23", (2) 2½" x 27"
Black (binding)	¼	Binding – (3) full-width 2½" strips

Constructing Date Night Tripper

1 Construct the nine Sawtooth Star blocks (see page 19).

2 Construct the 16 nine-patch blocks (see page 15). Before sewing, cut the 1½" full-width strips into smaller sections according to the number of three-square units needed, plus a couple of inches to allow for errors: 26" for 16 units, one full-width plus 11" for 32 units. Strip-piece the 1½" strips, press the seams away from the blue. Counter-cut them 1½" to create the three-square units. Join these units to complete the nine-patches.

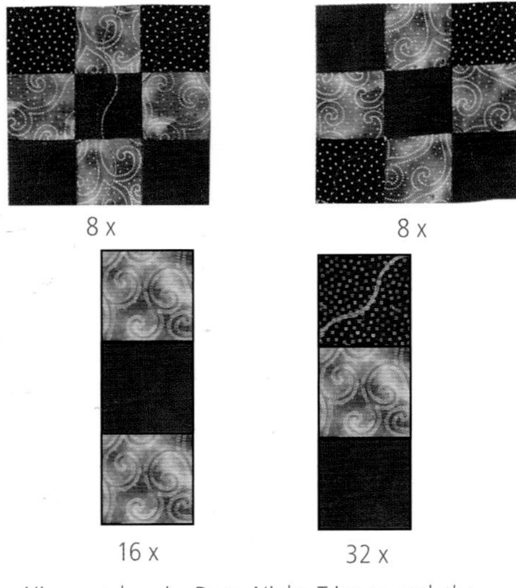

Nine-patches in Date Night Tripper and the three-square units required to make them

3 Construct the 16 Bowtie blocks (see page 18).

4 Construct the eight four-patch blocks (see page 15). Cut the full-width blue strip in half; stitch one half to the red 2" x 20" strip and the other half to the black 2" x 20" strip. Press the seams away from the blue. Counter-cut the strips 2" (eight of each type) and pair them together to make the four-patches.

5 Lay out the 49 blocks in the desired configuration and piece them in rows. Press the seams so that adjacent rows will abut in opposing directions. Assemble the rows (see page 25).

6 Add the 21½" inner borders to the sides and the 23" borders to the top and bottom. Repeat to add the 23" outer borders to the sides and the 27" outer borders to the top and bottom. Alternatively, miter the corners of the borders (see page 28).

7 Lay the quilt back flat, wrong side up on a firm surface. Place the batting on top of the backing and smooth out. Layer the quilt top, right-side up, over the backing. Baste the layers and quilt as desired. Like Spring Stars, the sample quilt features a diagonal grid of serpentine stitches.

8 Bind the quilt.

Day Tripper Totes

SKILL LEVEL: AVERAGE Make a tote bag for any occasion or season. The 9" composite block decorating each bag front is made from nine mini 3" blocks in a Trip Around the World format. There are four nine-patches, four Shoofly blocks, and one Ohio Star. Compare the bags and note how the pattern looks different when the colors and values are changed. This is an excellent small project for you to experiment and play with your own fabric combinations.

MATERIALS AND CUTTING FOR BLUE BAG

Optional: Use any 9" block

Materials	Yards	Cutting
Body and straps of bag (Light blue)	¾	(1) 17" x 30" (2) 3¾" x 33"
Borders (dark blue)	⅛	(2) 2" x 9½", (2) 2" x 11" from (1) full-width 2" strip
9" Block	Assorted small pieces	See page 46

MATERIALS AND CUTTING FOR THE NINE MINI-BLOCKS (BLUE BAG)

Block size: 3"

Note: If nine-patches are cut and made first, there will be enough leftover strips for most of the 1½" squares in other blocks.

Materials	Yards	Cutting
(1) Ohio Star block	Light blue	(4) 1½" squares, corner squares
	Dark blue	(1) 1½" square, center square
		(2) 2¼" squares, quarter-square triangles
	Pink	(1) 2¼" square, quarter-square triangles
	Green	(1) 2¼" square, quarter-square triangles
(4) Shoofly blocks	Light blue	(8) 1½" squares, side squares
	Dark blue	(8) 1½" squares, side squares
		(6) 2" squares, half-square triangles
	Pink	(4) 1½" squares, center squares
		(4) 2" squares, half-square triangles
	Green	(6) 2" squares, half-square triangles
(4) Nine-patches	All 4 colors	(1) full-width 1½" strip of each

Piece the Block

Use the photograph of the mini-blocks to help you position the colors, or insert your own fabric combinations. Photocopy and color the line drawing in Appendix 1 (see page 123) to help you plan. Make notes to stay organized and keep the fabrics in order.

1 Construct the four nine-patch blocks (see page 15). Cut 14" strips from the light blue, dark blue and green strips. Strip-piece, and counter-cut eight 1½" strips of squares. Cut one 8" strip from the dark blue and two 8" strips from the pink. Strip-piece and counter-cut four 1½" strips of squares. Join the strips of squares to complete the nine-patches.

2 Construct the Ohio Star block (see page 20). Make the quarter-square triangle units (see page 17) matching one dark blue square with the pink square and the other with the green square. Trim to 1½" and assemble with the squares to complete the block.

Composite 9" block and each mini-block

3 Construct the four Shoofly blocks (see page 19). Make the half-square triangle units (see page 16). Match two pink with dark blue squares, and the remaining two pink with green squares. Match the remaining four green squares with the four dark blues. You should have 16 half-square triangles. Trim to 1½" and assemble with the squares to complete the blocks.

4 Assemble the composite block from the nine mini-blocks. Make three rows, pressing the seams toward the nine-patches. Join the rows to complete the block.

Block Finishing and Bag Assembly

1 Fold the 9½" borders in half lengthwise with the right sides out and press. Attach the raw edges to the block sides. Press with the seams toward the border. Turn in each end of the 11" borders by ¼" toward the wrong side and press. Fold in half lengthwise and press. Attach to the top and bottom block edges. Make them fit exactly (adjust ¼" fold, if necessary) and backstitch at the beginning and end of the seams. Press the seams toward the border.

2 To appliqué, position the block on the tote bag body (17" x 30"), 2¾" from one of the 17" sides and 1¾" from the bottom edge. Pin in place and edgestitch around the border using either a straight stitch or a zigzag stitch. Use thread to match border or pick a contrasting color to make it more decorative.

3 Press a ¼" to ⅜" fold toward the wrong side on each of the strap long edges; press in half lengthwise with wrong sides together. Straight stitch or zigzag ⅛" from each edge, sewing the edge with the seam allowance folds first.

4 At the bag top edge, fold over ½" to the wrong side and press; fold again 1½" and press to make the hem fold. Unfold and sew the bag sides using a French seam (double seam so that raw edges are encased and not exposed). Refold the top edge and pin.

5 Insert and pin the strap ends under the hem fold 3" in from each bag side. (Place one strap on the bag front side and the other on the back.) Make sure that the straps are not twisted. Sew down the hem using a straight stitch and thread that matches the bag body. For added strength where the straps are tucked into the hem, sew a square and then diagonal lines in an "X" across the square.

6 Sew the bottom of the bag with a French seam.

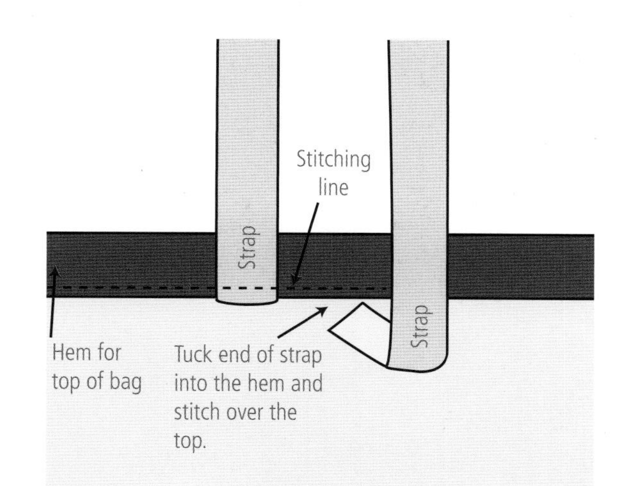

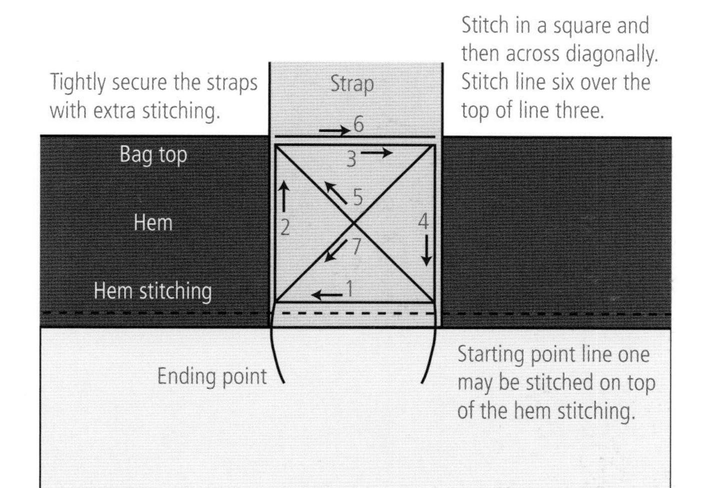

Basket of Fuchsias

Basket of Fuchsias pieced by the author, machine quilted by Wanda Rains (39" x 39")

SKILL LEVEL: AVERAGE In this charming wall hanging, Basket of Fuchsias, five block patterns merge together to create a striking overall design. Once again, the nine-patches provide the Trip Around the World framework. Interesting shapes appear from the juxtaposition of the black in the half-square triangles, nine-patches and Bowties. Linda Johnston's beautiful quilt, Trip Around the Woods, (page 51) is the same pattern with changes in the value placements yielding a totally different look.

MATERIALS FOR BASKET OF FUCHSIAS

Quilt size: 39" x 39" Block size: 4½"

Materials	Yards
Black (blocks, border)	1
Light rose (blocks, border)	¾
Green (blocks)	½
Pink (blocks, border)	½
Pink (binding)	½
Batting 42" x 42"	
Backing 42" x 42"	

To experiment with color and value placements, photocopy and color the line drawing of the quilt pattern found in Appendix 2 (see page 127).

CUTTING FOR BASKET OF FUCHSIAS

Blocks (total 49)	Color	Cutting
(8) Nine-patches	Pink	(1) full-width 2¾" strip
	Green	(1) full-width 2¾" strip
(5) Monkey Wrenches	Green	(5) 2" squares, center squares
	Black	(1) full-width 1¼" strip, side rectangles
		(10) 2½" squares, half-square triangles
	Light rose	(1) full-width 1¼" strip, side rectangles
		(10) 2½" squares, half-square triangles
(12) Bowties	Light rose	(24) 2¾" squares
		(24) 1½" squares
	Black	(24) 2¾" squares
(4) Half-square triangles	Green	(2) 5½" squares
	Black	(2) 5½" squares
(4) Quarter-square triangles	Green	(2) 5¾" squares
	Black	(2) 5¾" squares
(16) Nine-patches	Pink	(2) full-width 2" strips
	Green	(2) full-width 2" strips
	Black	(3) full-width 2" strips
	Light rose	(2) full-width 2" strips
Borders	Light rose	(4) full-width 1½" strips, inner border
	Pink	(4) full-width 1" strips, middle border
	Black	(4) full-width 2¾" strips, outer border

Constructing Basket of Fuchsias

1 Construct the four half-square triangles (see page 16); trim to 5".

2 Construct the four quarter-square triangles (see page 17); trim to 5".

3 Construct the eight four-patches (see page 15). Sew the two strips and counter-cut (16) 2¾". Join them in pairs to complete the blocks.

4 Construct the 12 bowtie blocks (see page 18).

5 Construct the five Monkey Wrench blocks (see Shoofly page 19). Note that the colors are reversed in one block. Join the 1¼" strips and counter-cut (20) 2" for the side rectangles. Make the 20 half-square triangles (see page 16); trim to 2". Assemble the components to complete the blocks.

6 Construct the 16 nine-patch blocks (see page 15). There are three different nine-patches, for which you'll need five strip sets. Before sewing, cut the full-width 2" strips into smaller sections according to the number of three-square units needed, plus a couple of inches to allow for errors: 10" for four units, 18" for eight units, 26" for 12 units, 35" for 16 units. Strip-piece the 2" strips. Press so that the seams abut and counter-cut them 2" to create the three-square units. Join these units to complete the nine-patches.

Nine-patches in Basket of Fuchsias and the three-square units required to make them

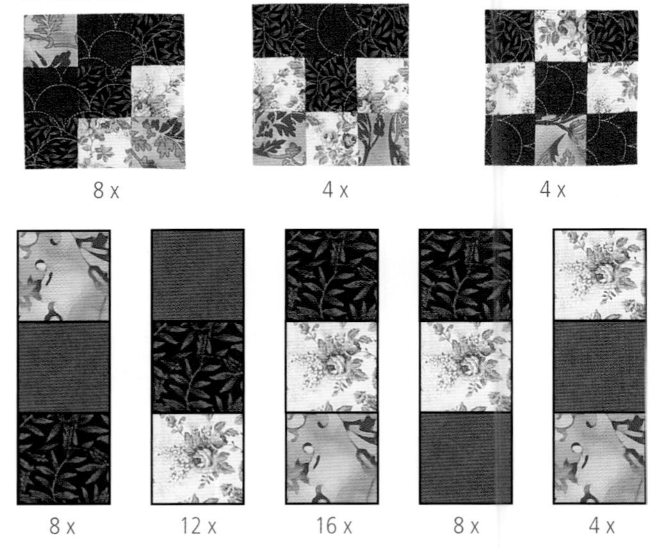

7 Assemble the quilt center field. Join the blocks in rows, pressing the seams away from the nine- and four-patches. Sew the rows together (see page 25).

8 Stitch the inner, middle and outer border strips together. Attach to the quilt top, mitering the corners (page 28). Alternatively, sew the borders on one at a time; first the sides and then the tops and bottoms (see table on next page for cutting sizes).

9 Lay the quilt back flat, wrong side up, on a firm surface. Place the batting on top of the backing and smooth out. Layer the quilt top, right-side up, over the backing. Baste the layers and quilt as desired. The sample quilt features an allover scallop stitch. This quilt lends itself well to a single allover pattern because the pattern and fabrics are fairly busy.

10 Bind the quilt.

CUTTING FOR BORDERS OF BASKET OF FUSCHIAS

Note: Unfinished size of quilt center field is 31½" x 31½". Check yours and adjust strip lengths, if necessary.

Border	Fabric	Cutting
Inner border strips	Rose	(2) 1½" x 31½," (2) 1½" x 33½"
Middle border strips	Pink	(2) 1" x 33½", (2) 1" x 34½"
Outer border strips	Black	(2) 2¾" x 34½", (2) 2¾" x 39"

Trip Around the Woods made by Linda W. Johnston (39" x 39") Photo by Mark Frey

Linda Johnston's quilt, Trip Around the Woods, makes an attractive accent on the wall of her living room. The pattern is the same, apart from the borders. The placement of light fabrics in the half-square and quarter-square triangles makes the pattern look remarkably different from Basket of Fuchsias. This is yet another example of how changing the value can dramatically alter the look of the pattern. Linda wanted to keep her tree fabric upright in the Bowties, so she constructed them with folded squares in the centers. Her quilting is simple straight lines outlining the patterns and moving diagonally across the blocks. The decorative loops for hanging the quilt, and the addition of ceramic tree buttons, add to the charm.

Trip Around the Garden

Trip Around the Garden pieced by the author, machine quilted by Wanda Rains (92" x 92")

SKILL LEVEL: AVERAGE The combination of floral and monochromatic prints creates a magical flower garden for a queen-sized bed. The colors cross the boundaries of the pieced blocks, sashing strips and cornerstones to maintain the integrity of the traditional Trip Around the World format and allow you to "walk" around the entire garden. This quilt is not difficult to piece. The main challenge lies in the fabric placement. There are plenty of opportunities for improvisation and you can use as many different floral fabrics as you like. This doesn't necessarily have to be a garden quilt. Use the format to place your fabrics as desired.

Trip Around the Garden has five different block styles with a total of 81 blocks, sashing with cornerstones, and six borders including the pieced piano keys. The 6" blocks are not complicated and the nine-patches are quick and easy to make.

MATERIALS FOR TRIP AROUND THE GARDEN

Quilt size: 92" x 92" Block size: 6"

Note: All fabrics appear in blocks and piano keys border. Additional positions are noted in parentheses.

Materials	Yards
Theme floral print (sashing, borders)	4½
Theme floral print (binding)	¾
Yellow mono (cornerstones, borders)	1½
Light green mono (cornerstones)	½
Dark green mono	¼
Burgundy mono (cornerstones)	1¼
Purple mono	¼
Mauve mono (cornerstones)	¼
Blue mono (cornerstones)	½
Mauve leaf print	¼
Light floral print (cornerstones)	½
Assorted floral prints (nine in sample quilt)	¼ of each
Batting 96" x 96"	
Backing 96" x 96"	

Cutting and Piecing for Blocks

NINE-PATCH BLOCKS

There are a total of 40 nine-patch blocks including six types arranged in tiers around the center in the Trip Around the World format. The inner tier is closest to the quilt center.

CUTTING FOR NINE-PATCH BLOCKS
Cut full-width 2½" strips as follows:
(9) Maroon
(8) Theme floral
(4) Dark green
(3) Yellow
(3) Mauve
(3) Mauve leaf
(2) Light floral
(2) Light green

Before sewing, cut the full-width 2½" strips into smaller sections according to the number of three-square units needed, plus a couple of inches to allow for errors: 12" for four units, 22" for eight units, 32" for 12 units, one full-width strip for 16 units. Leftover sections may be used later in the piano keys border. Piece one block type at a time, pressing the seams on the strips so that they will abut together nicely when assembled into the nine-patches. Counter-cut the strip sets 2½" to create the three-square units, then join the units to complete the nine-patches (see page 15).

Nine-patches in Trip Around the Garden and the three-square units required to make them

4 x

4 x

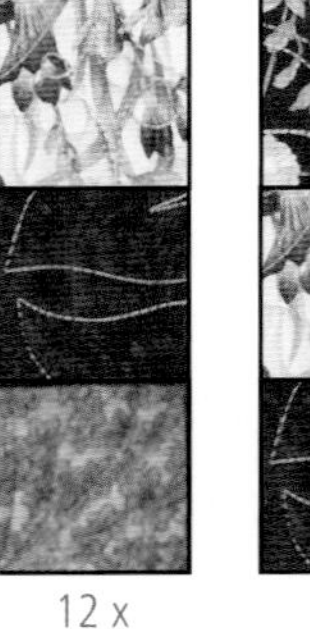

12 x

8 x

4 x

Inner tier

12 x

4 x

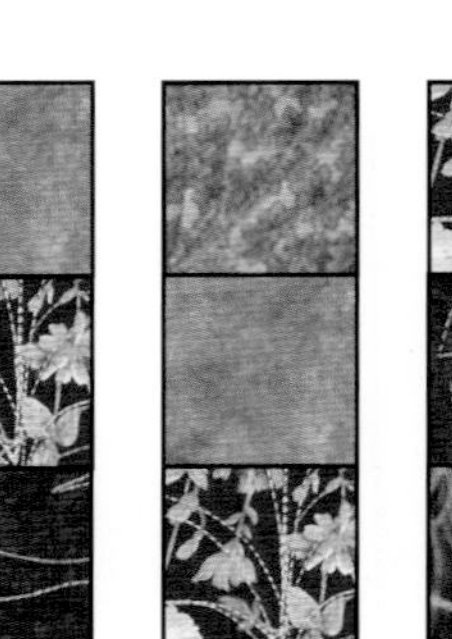

12 x

12 x

12 x

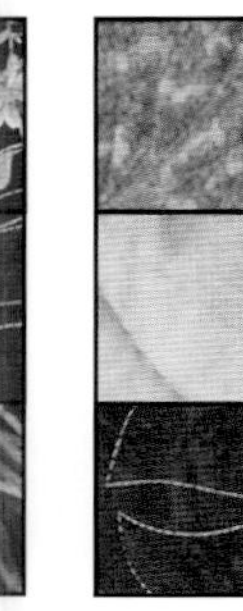

8 x

4 x

Middle tier

Outer tier
12 x

Outer corner
4 x

12 x

12 x

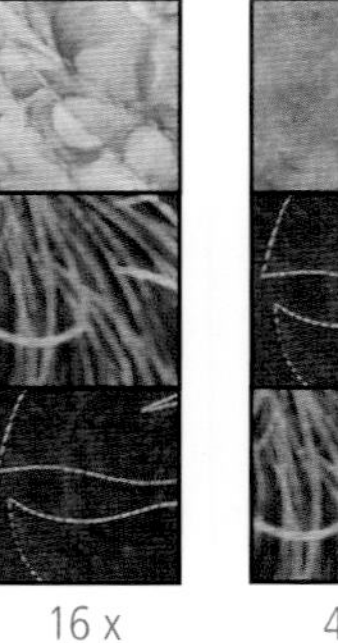

16 x

4 x

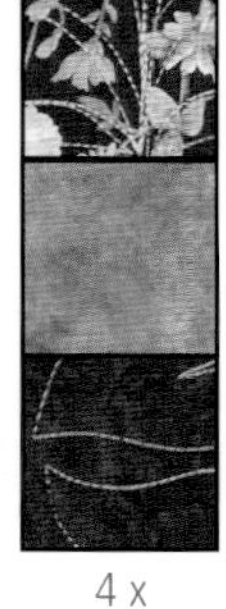

4 x

Outer tier

OHIO STAR BLOCKS

The four Ohio Star blocks have two background colors — yellow and light green. The blocks are all the same, but set in a way that forms a secondary pattern extending across their boundaries and forming a large on-point green area in the middle of the quilt. I fussy cut the pansies in the center squares and oriented them to face toward the center. If you're particular about such details, pay attention when piecing the blocks to achieve the desired effect. Piece the four Ohio Star blocks. Make the quarter-square triange units (see page 17). Pair the maroon squares with the light green and yellow squares - see photo above for layout, carefully trim them to 2½" and join with the squares to complete the block (see page 20).

CUTTING FOR OHIO STAR BLOCKS

Block part	Fabric	Cutting
Center squares	Pansy	(4) 2½" squares
Star points (quarter-square triangles)	Maroon	(8) 3¼" squares
	Light green	(5) 3¼" squares
	Yellow	(3) 3¼" squares
Corner squares	Yellow	(8) 2½" squares
	Light green	(8) 2½" squares

BOWTIE BLOCKS

Make eight Bowtie blocks. The sample quilt features two different pansy fabrics with two purple backgrounds (four of each). Construct the Bowties (see page 18).

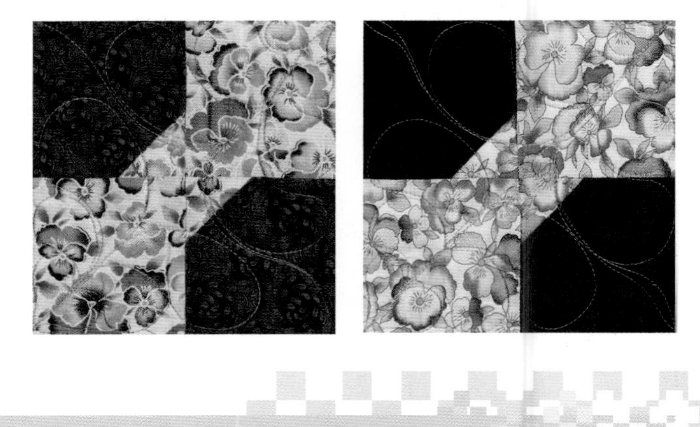

CUTTING FOR BOWTIE BLOCKS

Block Part	Fabric	Cutting
Large squares	Background fabric	(16) 3½" squares
Large Squares	Bowtie fabric	(16) 3½" squares
Corner Square Triangles	Bowtie fabric	(16) 1¾" squares

SHOOFLY BLOCKS

Make 12 Shoofly blocks. My quilt has four each in three small floral prints. Begin by strip piecing the center three-square units of the blocks from the maroon and blue strips. Press the seams away from the center maroon strip and counter-cut the strip set (12) 2½". Construct the half-square triangles units (see page 16); carefully trim to 2½". Complete the blocks (see page 19).

CUTTING FOR SHOOFLY BLOCKS

Block part	Fabric	
Center three-square units	Maroon Blue	(1) 2½" x 28" strip (2) 2½" x 28" strips
Side squares	Blue	(24) 2½" squares
Half-square triangle units	Blue	(24) 3" squares
	Floral	(24) 3" squares (optional: 8 each of 3 fabrics)

SAWTOOTH STAR BLOCKS

There are 17 Sawtooth Star blocks, 16 on yellow and one in the center with a light green background and fussy-cut pansies in the middle. Of the 16 blocks, eight feature freesia fabric (light floral) and eight feature pansies (four each of two pansy fabrics). Piece the Sawtooth Stars (see page 19).

CUTTING FOR SAWTOOTH STAR BLOCKS

Block part	Fabric	Cutting
Center squares	Dark floral (pansy)	(1) 3½" square
	Light floral	(16) 3½" squares (optional: use variety of fabrics)
Background corner squares	Light green	(4) 2" squares
	Yellow	(64) 2" squares
Background side rectangles	Light green	(4) 2" x 3½"
	Yellow	(64) 2" x 3½"
Star points	Maroon	(136) 2" squares

Constructing Trip Around the Garden

The quilt is designed so that the blocks and sashing strips blend together into an overall pattern. To achieve this, the sashing floral fabric was used in the nine-patches, and the colors of the cornerstones were chosen carefully to carry across the boundaries of the blocks.

Before cutting into the sashing fabric, cut the border strips lengthwise from 94" of the fabric. They will be trimmed to the correct length before attaching to the quilt top. On the sample quilt, the side strips were cut lengthwise, and the top and bottom were cut crosswise and joined to match. Here the flowers and foliage are all oriented the same way, and likewise for the sashing strips. If your fabric doesn't have a particular direction, or you are not worried about this, cut all 12 strips lengthwise so that you don't have seams. The yellow border strips can be cut crosswise and joined, because the seams are barely visible on the monochromatic fabric.

This quilt has six borders.
First border - yellow
Second border - floral theme
Third border - piano keys
Fourth border - floral theme
Fifth border - yellow
Sixth border - floral theme

CUTTING FOR SASHING, CORNERSTONES AND BORDERS

Note: Cut long second, fourth, and sixth border strips before sashing.

Border part	Fabric	Cutting
Second and fourth borders	Theme floral	(8) 2" x 94" cut lengthwise
Sixth border	Theme floral	(4) 3½" x 94" cut lengthwise
Sashing strips	Theme floral	(180) 2" x 6½"
Cornerstones (total 100)	Yellow	(40) 2" squares
	Maroon	(24) 2" squares
	Mauve	(12) 2" squares
	Blue	(12) 2" squares
	Light floral	(8) 2" squares
	Light green	(4) 2" squares
First and fifth borders	Yellow	(17) full-width 1" strips (join strips and trim to size)
Second and fourth border cornerstones	Yellow	(8) 2" square
Piano keys border (third border)	All fabrics	Assorted 1½", 1¾" and 2" x 4¾" strips
Sawtooth Stars (at corners of piano keys border)		
Center squares	Pansy	(4) 2½" squares (Optional: Fussy cut)
Background rectangles	Light green	(16) 1½" x 2½"
Background corner squares	Light green	(16) 1½" squares
Star points	Maroon	(32) 1½" squares

1 Assemble the center field of the quilt (see pages 25-27). Lay out the blocks, sashing strips and cornerstones in the correct configuration. Use the photograph of the quilt as a guide, or arrange them in your own pattern. Piece the center field of the quilt by joining the blocks, sashing and cornerstones in rows, pressing the seams toward the sashing strips, and then sewing the rows together.

2 The center field should measure 69½" x 69½". Measure yours in both directions across the middle, and make adjustments to the border strips if necessary (see page 28).

3 First border - yellow: Add the 1" x 69½" borders to the sides, then add the 1" x 70½" borders to the top and bottom, or miter the corners (see page 28).

4 Second border - floral theme: Trim four of the 2"-wide 94"-long floral strips to 70½". Sew two strips onto the quilt sides. Add cornerstones to the ends of the remaining two strips. Join these to the top and bottom of the quilt top.

5 Third border - piano keys: Make the piano keys border using as many of the fabrics as desired (see page 22). The featured quilt uses a total of 19 fabrics. Sixteen strips of each were cut and joined in pairs at random. Then the pieced sections were added together. At each end a 2" floral fabric strip was used, so that all the corner stars are framed by the same fabric. Make the four piano keys borders 73½" long. Trim them to a width of 4½". Piece the Sawtooth Stars for the corners (see page 19). Attach the borders and corners in the same manner as the previous border.

6 Fourth border - floral theme: Trim the remaining four 2"-wide 94"-long floral strips to 81½". Sew a yellow cornerstone to each end of two borders. Join the borders to the quilt in the same manner as the previous borders.

7 Fifth border - yellow: Add the fifth narrow border using two 1" x 84½" and two 1" x 85½" strips.

8 Sixth border - floral theme: Add the final 3½" floral border, using two strips 3½" x 85½" and two 3½" x 91½". Alternatively, miter the corners of the fifth and sixth borders together (see page 28).

9 Lay the quilt back flat, wrong side up, on a firm surface. Place the batting on top of the backing and smooth out. Layer the quilt top, right-side up, over the backing. Baste the layers and quilt as desired. Quilter, Wanda Rains, custom quilted the featured quilt on her long-arm quilting machine with beautiful floral patterns and large feathers in the piano keys border.

10 Add the binding.

Tripping Pinwheels

Christmas Roses Around the World designed by the author, pieced by Joanne Bennett, machine quilted by Wanda Rains (80" x 67")

In Christmas Roses Around the World, the Trip Around the World squares are enlarged and subdivided into half-square triangle, quarter-square triangle and on-point Pinwheel blocks. The on-point pattern sequence is maintained and allows the eye to travel around this attractive quilt.

1920s Ohio Star from the collection
of Joe and Mary Koval

CHAPTER FOUR

Ohio Star

Oh-Just Do It! designed and pieced by Susan Burker, machine quilted by Barbara Dau (87" x 87") Photo by Mark Frey

I love the versatility of the Ohio Star. There are so many different ways to color and shade the star and it looks terrific either as a light star on a dark background or vice versa. The patterns featured alter the star in a variety of ways. The first simply enlarges it to a 27" block. Next, I've designed a new block that I call the Tweaked Ohio Star, which has extra triangles and a pieced frame. I've explored several options using this block to create new patterns, and you'll see what a difference value placement and settings can make. In the final project, I've inserted a skinny lattice into the star block, a technique that can be used on any nine- or four-patch block.

Another option is to use a variety of sizes of stars overlapping. This is beautifully illustrated in Susan Burker's stunning quilt, which includes stars ranging in size from 3" to 81".

Look at the wonderful way that the small stars shine through the transparent large star. (Susan proudly told me that she had all those shades of green in her fabric stash and didn't buy any new ones for this quilt.) The fabric placement is superb and required much time and planning on graph paper and on the work wall before Susan was satisfied.

Large Ohio Star

SKILL LEVEL: EASY This enlarged Ohio Star is easy to make for a cozy lap quilt or decorative wall hanging. I've made it three times - in brightly colored flannels, whimsical flowers and dragonflies with a fleece back, and with printed ferns and ornate quilting. It's an excellent quick project and one that young quilters would enjoy.

Bright Star, flannel top and back, made by the author (51" x 51")

MATERIALS AND CUTTING FOR BRIGHT STAR, (FLANNEL OHIO STAR)

Quilt size: 51" x 51" Block size: 27"

Materials	Yards	Cutting
Orange (star, border corners)	¾	(1) 9½" square, center
		(2) 10¼" squares, star points
		(4) 3½" squares, corners for inner border
		(4) 9½" squares, corners for outer border
Turquoise (star background)	⅔	(4) 9½" squares, block corners
		(2) 10¼" squares, quarter-square triangles
Blue (outer side panels)	1	(4) 9½" x 33½" cut lengthwise
Purple (inner border)	½	(4) 3½" x 27½" strips, inner border
Purple (binding)	½	
Batting 55" x 55"		
Backing 55" x 55"		

Aruinzaya's Quilt, fleece back with no batting, made by the author (51" x 51")
Photo by Mark Frey

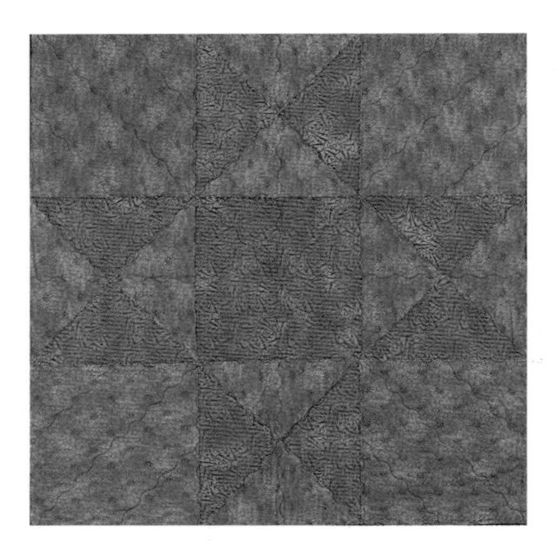

Constructing Bright Star

1 Piece the block beginning with the quarter-square triangle units to make the star points (see page 17). Trim to 9½". Complete the blocks (see page 20).

2 Attach the two inner side borders, then sew cornerstones to the short ends of the remaining two inner borders. Sew them to the quilt top and bottom. Repeat the steps to attach the outer border.

3 Lay the quilt back flat, wrong side up, on a firm surface. Place the batting on top of the backing and smooth out. Layer the quilt top, right-side up, over the backing. Baste the layers and quilt as desired. For the flannel quilt, the binding strips were cut 3" wide rather than 2½" to allow for the extra bulk of the flannel. The featured quilt was quilted with serpentine stitches in diagonal lines. Aruinzaya's Quilt also has serpentine stitches, a fleece backing and no batting.

Ferntastic Star was made for a Kitsap Quilters' Guild challenge. The black floral fabric was provided by the Guild, and the challenge was simply "star" — any interpretation. I picked ferns from my yard and printed them onto the yellow background fabric using textile paint. I quilted the ferns in green glossy rayon thread to accentuate the fronds and stipple quilted around the flowers in the floral star.

Ferntastic Star, ferns printed with textile paint, made by the author (51" x 51")

Tweaked Ohio Star The Block Pattern

The Tweaked Ohio Star is a new 12" block that I created by substituting the corner squares of the star with half-square triangles and adding a pieced frame. It's remarkably versatile, as you'll see from the next five projects. Like the traditional Ohio Star, there are many interesting ways to color and shade the block that make it change dramatically in appearance. The Ohio Star may be set on-point or the octagon of triangles surrounding the star highlighted. A variety of options are well illustrated in the nine-block sampler, Stars at Sunset.

Photocopy the line drawing in Appendix 3 (see page 125) and experiment with coloring the blocks in different ways. Alternatively, if available, use computer software such as Electric Quilt to draw and color the block.

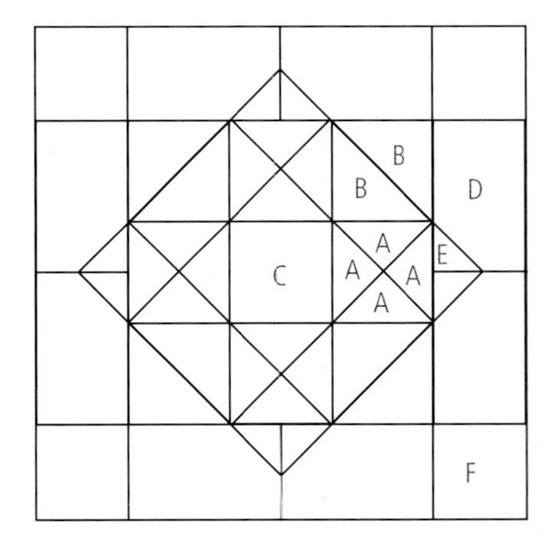

A - Star points (quarter-square triangles)
B - Half-square triangles
C - Center square
D - Framing strip
E - Triangle for framing strip
F - Outer corner

Constructing the Tweaked Ohio Star Block

Construct the Ohio Stars with half-square triangle corners; then add the frames.

Note that the sides of the frames are pieced, so take care to select fabrics that will not show the seams. Using small prints or monochromatic fabrics is recommended, because the seams may be more obvious with large prints.

Light star on dark background

Dark star on light background

CUTTING FOR ONE TWEAKED OHIO STAR BLOCK USING TWO COLORS

Block size: 12"

Block parts	Fabric A	Fabric B
Star points (quarter-square triangles)	(2) 3¾" squares	(2) 3¾" squares
Half-square triangles	(2) 3½" squares	(2) 3½" squares
Center square	(1) 3" square	
Framing strips	(8) 2¾" x 4¼"	
Triangles for framing strips		(8) 1¾" squares
Outer corners		(4) 2¾" squares

1 Piece the quarter-square triangle star point units (see page 17). Trim to 3".

2 Piece the half-square triangle corner units (see page 16). Trim to 3".

3 Join the squares in rows, as for the regular Ohio Star (see page 20). Press the seams toward the quarter-square triangle units. Stitch the rows together.

4 Make the small triangles on the framing strips by using the corner-square triangle method (see page 15). Take care when placing the triangles, because mirror images are needed for each side (four attached to lower left corners and four attached to lower right corners). Join one of each to make the framing strips and press the seams open. Sew them onto the star with the corner squares to complete the block. Refer to the diagrams to help you.

STEP-BY-STEP CONSTRUCTION OF THE TWEAKED OHIO STAR BLOCK

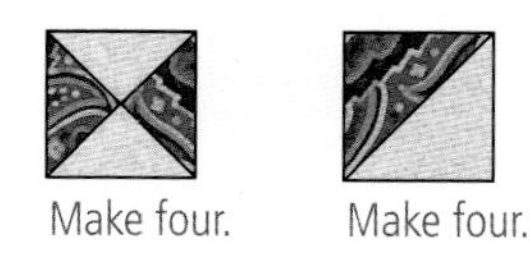

Make four. Make four.

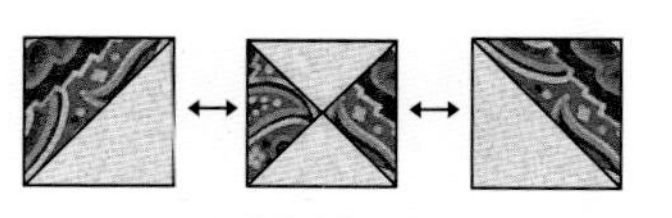

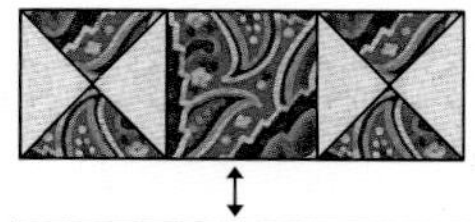

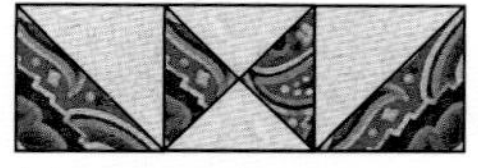

Join squares in rows.
Assemble rows.

Completed center of block

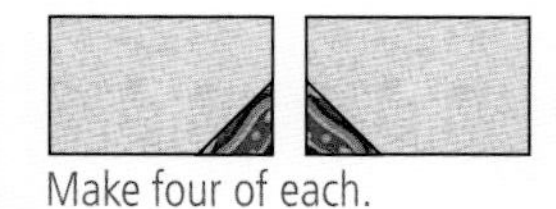

Make four of each.

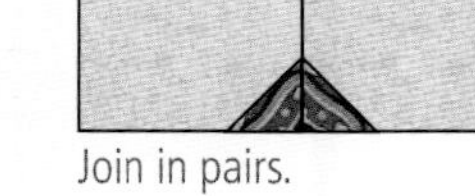

Join in pairs.

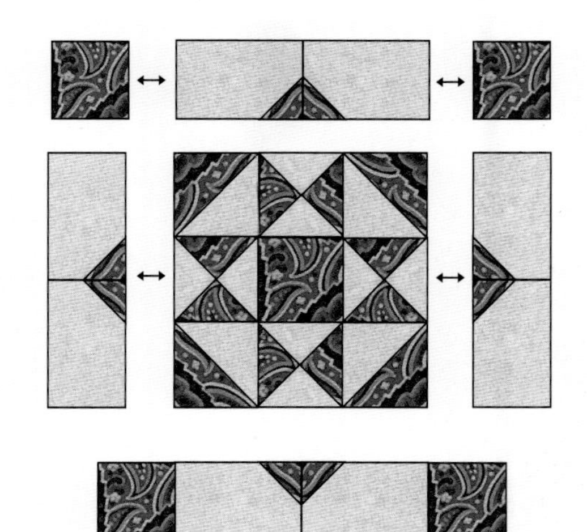

Join pieces in rows. Assemble rows to complete block.

When piecing the half and quarter blocks that appear at the sides and in the corners of Tutti Fruity and Queen's Courtyard, note that there are half half-square triangles, half corner squares, and half and quarter center squares. For the half half-square triangles, piece them as for regular half-square triangle units but do not trim them. Cut them in half diagonally as you would when making quarter-square triangles. Your starting squares will be slightly larger to accommodate the seam allowances and the sizes are provided with the patterns. The same construction order applies as for the whole block. Take extra care to prevent distortion of the bias edges of these partial blocks.

HALF TWEAKED OHIO STAR BLOCK FOR SETTING TRIANGLES

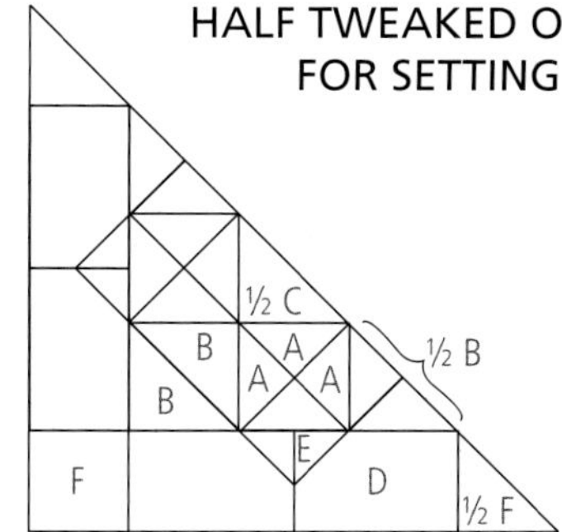

A: Star points (quarter-square triangles)
B: Half-square triangles
½ B: ½ half-square triangles
½ C: ½ center square
D: Framing strip
E: Triangle for framing strip
F: Outer corner
½ F: half outer corner

Light star, dark background

Dark star, light background

QUARTER TWEAKED OHIO STAR BLOCK FOR CORNER TRIANGLES

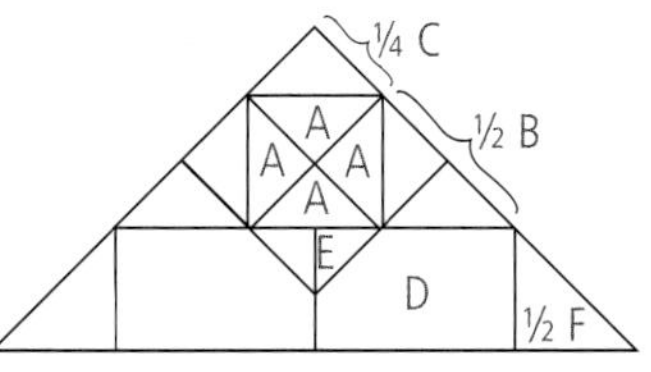

A: Star points (quarter-square triangles)
½ B: half half-square triangles
¼ C: quarter center square
D: Framing strip
E: Triangle for framing strip
½ F: half outer corner

Dark star, light background

Light star, dark background

Tweaked Ohio Star Pillows

SKILL LEVEL: EASY These attractive 18" pillows may be accents for a living room or made to match a bedroom quilt. This simple cover has two overlapping back pieces and no snaps, buttons or zippers. The pillows are quick to piece and are a good way to practice constructing the block before you embark on a larger project.

MATERIALS AND CUTTING

Pillow size: 18" x 18"Block size: 12"

Materials	Yards	Cutting
Tweaked Ohio Star block	Assorted small pieces (See page 66)	
Inner border	⅛	(2) 1" x 12½" sides
		(2) 1 x 13½" top and bottom
Outer borders and pillow back	¾	(4) 3¼" x 13½" sides
		(2) 2¾" x 19" top and bottom
		(2) 12½" x 19" pillow back
Cornerstones for outer border	⅛	(4) 3¼" squares
Pillow form - 18" square		

Constructing the Pillow

1 Construct the Tweaked Ohio Star block (see page 65). Use your own combination of fabrics. Experiment by photocopying and coloring the line drawing found in Appendix 3 (see page 125). Alternatively, use any other 12" block.

2 Attach the inner borders to the sides, then the top and bottom. Attach the outer borders to the sides. Sew the cornerstones to short ends of the remaining two outer borders. Sew these to the top and bottom of the block.

3 Press under ¼" on one backing piece long edge. Press under again ½". Sew to secure using a thread color that matches the fabric. Repeat on the remaining back piece.

4 Lay the pillow top right-side up on the table and place the backing pieces over it, right sides down, so that they overlap at least 2½" with the hemmed folds in the middle. Align the outer raw edges of the pillow tops and backs and pin. Stitch around the edge with a ⅜" seam allowance. Clip the corners before turning right sides out. Insert the pillow form.

Place right sides of pillow front and backs together. Clip corners before turning right sides out.

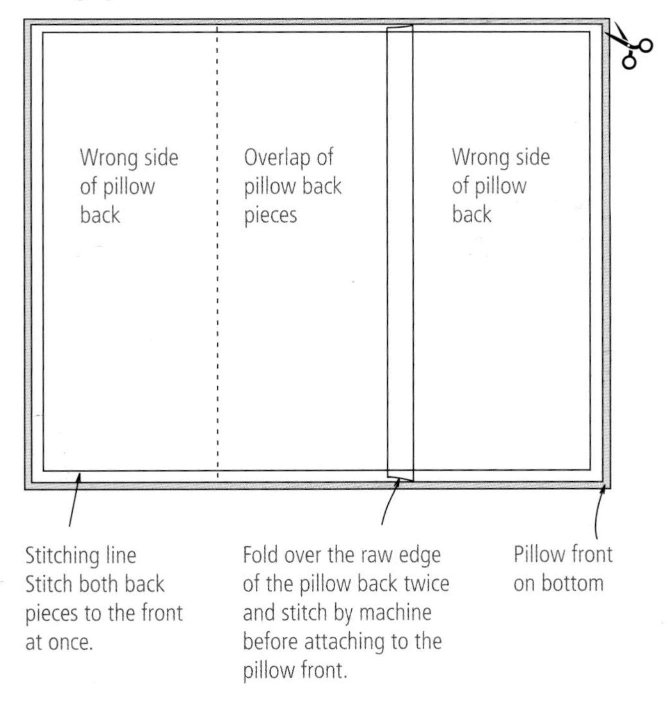

Nine-Block Sampler - Stars at Sunset

Stars at Sunset pieced by the author, machine quilted by Wanda Rains (50½" x 50½").

SKILL LEVEL: AVERAGE This stunning lap quilt illustrates a variety of presentations for the Tweaked Ohio Star block. Have fun creating your own coloring and value placements in this versatile block. Remember that adjacent pieces can be of the same fabric, as demonstrated in four of the blocks in Stars at Sunset.

MATERIALS FOR STARS AT SUNSET

Quilt size: 50½" x 50½"   Block size: 12"

Materials	Yards
Dark blue/purple (blocks, cornerstones, borders)	1
Light yellow/orange (blocks, borders)	1
Light blue (blocks, sashing, borders)	¾
Gray/brown (blocks, borders)	¾
Tan/brown (blocks, borders)	½
Orange/multi swirl (blocks, borders)	½
Orange/multi swirl (binding)	½
Batting 54" x 54"	
Backing 54" x 54"	

CUTTING FOR STARS AT SUNSET

Note: See Appendices 3 and 4 on pages 125-126 for planning the blocks. See page 66 for cutting the block pieces. Check the measurements of the center field before cutting the border strips and adjust, if necessary.

Quilt parts	Fabric	Cutting
Blocks (9)	Assorted	See page 66
Sashing	Light blue	(16) 1½" x 12½"
Sashing	Orange/multi swirl	(8) 1½" x 12½"
Cornerstones	Dark blue/purple	(16) 1½" squares
Inner border	Light yellow/orange	(4) 2" x 40½"
Inner border cornerstones	Dark blue/purple	(4) 2" squares
Middle border	Dark blue/purple	(2) 1" x 43½", (2) 1" x 44½"
Pieced outer border	Light blue	(4) 3½" x 15¼"
Pieced outer border	Gray/brown	(4) 3½" x 15¼"
Pieced outer border	Tan/brown	(4) 3½" x 7¾"
Pieced outer border	Light yellow/orange	(4) 3½" x 7¾"
Outer border cornerstones	Dark blue/purple	(4) 3½" squares

Constructing Stars at Sunset

1 Construct the nine blocks as desired. Look at the photo or create your own patterns using different value placements. Photocopy the line drawing in Appendix 3 (see page 125) and color your own blocks. Record the fabric placements for the nine blocks in Appendix 4 (see page 126). This will help you stay organized as you cut all the components. For further cutting and piecing instructions see pages 65-67.

2 Assemble the blocks, sashing, and cornerstones (see pages 25-27).

3 Attach the borders (see page 28). Before adding each one, check the quilt top measurements and adjust the size as necessary. The unfinished center field, without borders, should be 40½" x 40½". After adding the middle border, it should be 44½" x 44½". If it's different, adjust the length of the 7¾" border sections.

4 Lay the quilt back flat, wrong side up, on a firm surface. Place the batting on top of the backing and smooth out. Layer the quilt top, right-side up, over the backing. Baste the layers and quilt as desired. Quilter Wanda Rains quilted an overall pattern of waves and swirls, reminiscent of rippling water.

5 Add the binding.

Tutti Fruity

Tutti Fruity designed by the author and made by Gladys Schulz (61" x 61")

SKILL LEVEL: CHALLENGING This vibrant large lap quilt features strawberry and blueberry fabrics along with orange and plum colors. The jazzy striped border is a lively addition to the on-point Tweaked Ohio Star blocks. Make a scrappy quilt with as many fabrics as you like, or use just two fabrics, for example, blue and white to make a more classic looking quilt.

The quilt is made from on-point blocks alternating in value placement. There are nine blocks with light backgrounds and dark stars, and four blocks with dark backgrounds and light stars. The eight half-blocks on the sides and four quarter-blocks in the corners are all dark backgrounds with light partial stars. These half and quarter blocks present the most challenging part of the quilt because of the bias edges. You'll need to take extra care to avoid stretching the sides when adding the borders.

Use as many different light and dark fabrics as desired. Quilt designer, Gladys Schulz, used the same light fabric throughout, and a variety of darks in the blocks. The pattern is complex. I recommend cutting and piecing each group of blocks separately.

MATERIALS FOR TUTTI FRUITY

Quilt size: 61" x 61" Block size: 12"

Materials	Yards
Light for blocks	2¼
One or several darks for blocks (total)	2
Inner border	½
Outer border	¾
Binding	⅔
Batting 64" x 64"	
Backing 64" x 64"	

CUTTING FOR TUTTI FRUITY

Note: See page 66 for cutting single blocks. Asterisked figures are number of full-width 42" strips required to yield pieces. If there is no figure, one strip or leftovers from strips previously cut will be sufficient.

Block parts	Light fabric	Dark Fabric
(9) blocks with light backgrounds and dark stars		
Star points (quarter-square triangles)	(18) 3¾" squares - *2	(18) 3¾" squares - *2
Half-square triangles	(18) 3½" squares - *2	(18) 3½" squares - *2
Center squares		(9) 3" squares
Framing strips	(72) 2¾" x 4¼" - *6 @ 2¾"	
Triangles for framing strips		(72) 1¾" squares - *4
Outer corners		(36) 2¾" squares - *3
(4) blocks with dark backgrounds and light stars		
Star points (quarter-square triangles)	(8) 3¾" squares	(8) 3¾" squares
Half-square triangles	(8) 3½" squares	(8) 3½" squares
Center squares	(4) 3" squares	
Framing strips		(32) 2¾" x 4¼" - *4 @ 2¾"
Triangles for framing strips	(32) 1¾" squares - *2	
Outer corners	(16) 2¾" squares - *2	
(8) half-blocks for sides		
Star points (quarter-square triangles)	(8) 3¾" squares	(8) 3¾" squares
Half-square triangles	(4) 3½" squares	(4) 3½" squares
½ half-square triangles	(4) 3¾" squares	(4) 3¾" squares
½ center squares	(4) 3⅜" squares cut in half diagonally	
Framing strips		(32) 2¾" x 4¼" -*4 @ 2¾"
Triangles for framing strips	(32) 1¾" squares *2	
Outer corners	(8) 2¾" squares	
½ outer corners	(8) 3⅛" squares cut in half diagonally	
(4) quarter-blocks for corners		
Star points (quarter-square triangles)	(2) 3¾" squares	(2) 3¾" squares
½ half-square triangles	(2) 3¾" squares	(2) 3¾" squares
¼ center squares	(1) 3¾" square cut diagonally both ways	
Framing strips		(8) 2¾" x 4¼"
Triangles for framing strips	(8) 1¾" squares	
½ outer corners	(4) 3⅛" squares cut in half diagonally	
Borders (Measure quilt before cutting exact length; adjust, if necessary.)		
Inner border	(2) 2" x 51½"	
	(2) 2" x 54½"	
Outer border		(2) 4" x 54½"
		(2) 4" x 61½"

Constructing Tutti Fruity

1 Construct the 13 whole Tweaked Ohio Star blocks and the 12 partial blocks (see pages 65-67). Press the seams on the frames toward the dark fabrics, then seams on adjacent blocks will abut nicely when quilt top is assembled.

2 Assemble the blocks and partial blocks in diagonal rows (see page 27-28).

3 The quilt top should measure 51½" x 51½". Check yours and adjust the length of the border strips if necessary (see page 28).

4 Add the inner borders to the right and left sides, then the top and bottom. Repeat for the outer borders. Pin and sew carefully to maintain all the triangle points on the center field and avoid warping the bias edges.

5 Lay the quilt back flat, wrong side up, on a firm surface. Place the batting on top of the backing and smooth out. Layer the quilt top, right-side up, over the backing. Baste the layers and quilt as desired. Quilt designer Gladys Schulz quilted the center field using two, pretty, alternating curved patterns placed so that one loopy formation appears in the middles of all the on-point blocks and the other is centered over the four-patches where the block corners meet. The border features a pattern of curves and hearts.

6 Add the binding.

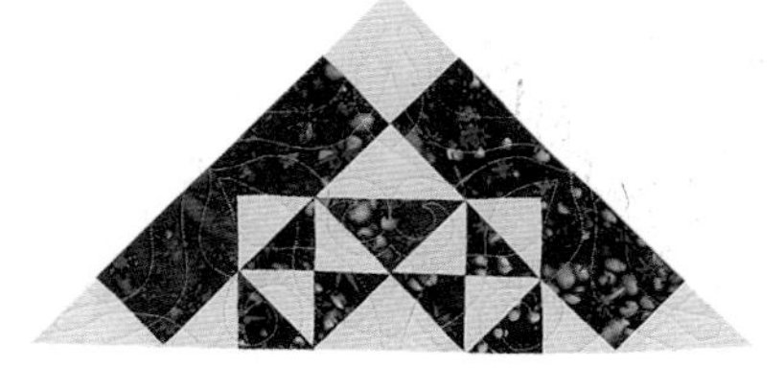

Queen's Courtyard

Queen's Courtyard pieced by the author, machine quilted by Wanda Rains (90" x 90")

SKILL LEVEL: CHALLENGING Queen's Courtyard is a clean, sharp-looking pattern, reminding me of a tiled floor. This queen-sized quilt is an expansion of the previous pattern, Tutti Fruity, with sashing strips, cornerstones and more intricate coloring. The sashing adds new dimension and interesting secondary patterns emerge with the intersecting cornerstones and the block outer corners.

Like Tutti Fruity, Queen's Courtyard consists of on-point blocks alternating in value placement, but sashing strips also are included. There are 16 blocks with red stars on light backgrounds and nine blocks with light stars on dark backgrounds, five with red centers and four with yellow centers. The light stars are not so obvious and look more like dark hourglasses. The half-blocks on the sides and the quarter-blocks in the corners continue this pattern sequence with light stars on dark backgrounds.

MATERIALS FOR QUEEN'S COURTYARD

Quilt size: 90" x 90" Block size: 12"

Materials	Yards
Blue (blocks, sashing and border)	3 (Optional: Use more than one blue)
Black (blocks and border)	3¼
White (blocks)	2¾
Yellow (blocks)	1
Red (blocks and cornerstones)	1½
Red (binding)	¾
Batting 94" x 94"	
Backing 94" x 94"	

CUTTING FOR QUEEN'S COURTYARD

Note: Begin by cuttng the black and blue long border strips lengthwise from fabric. Asterisked figures are number of full-width 42" strips required to yield pieces. If there is no figure, one strip or leftovers from strips previously cut will be sufficient. Cutting and piecing each group of blocks separately is recommended.

Quilt parts	Fabric	Pieces
(16) blocks with red stars on light backgrounds		
Star points (quarter-square triangles)	Red	(32) 3¾" squares - *4
Star points (quarter-square triangles)	Yellow	(16) 3¾" squares - *2
Star points (quarter-square triangles)	White	(16) 3¾" squares - *2
Half-square triangles	Yellow	(32) 3½" squares - *3
Half-square triangles	Black	(32) 3½" squares - *3
Center squares	Black	(16) 3" squares - *2
Framing strips	White	(128) 2¾" x 4¼" - *10 @ 2¾"
Triangles for framing strips	Black	(128) 1¾" squares - *6
Cornerstones	Black	(64) 2¾" squares - *5
(9) blocks with white stars on dark backgrounds (five with red centers, four with yellow centers)		
Star points (quarter-square triangles)	White	(18) 3¾" squares - *2
Star points (quarter-square triangles)	Black	(18) 3¾" squares -*2
Half-square triangles	White	(18) 3½" squares - *2
Half-square triangles	Blue	(18) 3½" squares - *2
Center squares	Red	(5) 3" squares
Center squares	Yellow	(4) 3" squares
Framing strips	Black	(72) 2¾" x 4¼" - *6 @ 2¾"
Triangles for framing strips	White	(72) 1¾" squares - *4
Cornerstones	Red	(36) 2¾" squares - *3

Quilt parts	Fabric	Pieces
(12) half-blocks for sides (eight with yellow centers, four with red centers)		
Star points (quarter-square triangles)	White	(12) 3¾" squares
Star points (quarter-square triangles)	Black	(12) 3¾" squares
Half-square triangles	White	(6) 3½" squares
Half-square triangles	Blue	(6) 3½" squares
½ half-square triangles	White	(6) 3¾" squares
½ half-square triangles	Blue	(6) 3¾" squares
½ center squares	Yellow	(4) 3⅜" squares cut in half diagonally
½ center squares	Red	(2) 3⅜" squares cut in half diagonally
Framing strips	Black	(48) 2¾" x 4¼" - *4 @ 2¾"
Triangles for framing strips	White	(48) 1¾" squares - *3
Outer corners	Red	(12) 2¾" squares
½ outer squares	Red	(12) 3⅛" squares cut in half diagonally
(4) quarter-blocks for corners		
Star points (quarter-square triangles)	White	(2) 3¾" squares
Star points (quarter-square triangles)	Black	(2) 3¾" squares
½ half-square triangles	Blue	(2) 3¾" squares
½ half-square triangles	White	(2) 3¾" squares
¼ center squares	Red	(1) 3¾" square cut diagonally both ways
Framing strips	Black	(8) 2¾" x 4¼"
Triangles for framing strips	White	(8) 1¾" squares
½ outer corners	Red	(4) 3⅛" squares cut in half diagonally
Sashing, cornerstones and borders		
Sashing	Blue	(64) 2½" x 12½" - cut after border strips
Cornerstones	Red	(24) 2½" squares, - *2
½ sashing cornerstones on sides	Red	(8) 2⅞" squares cut in half diagonally
Inner borders	Black	(4) 2½" x 90"
Outer borders	Blue	(4) 4" x 92"

Constructing Queen's Courtyard

1 Construct the 25 whole Tweaked Ohio Star blocks and 16 partial blocks (see page 65-67). Take extra care when handling the bias edges on the partial blocks to ensure they aren't stretched or distorted.

2 Assemble the blocks, partial blocks, sashing strips and cornerstones in diagonal rows (see page 27-28).

3 Sew each of the inner and outer borders together. Attach each set to the center field, mitering the corners (see page 28).

4 Lay the quilt back flat, wrong side up, on a firm surface. Place the batting on top of the backing and smooth out. Layer the quilt top, right-side up, over the backing. Baste the layers and quilt as desired. Quilter Wanda Rains quilted an overall plume pattern. The striking pieced design lends itself well to overall quilting patterns.

5 Add the binding.

Tropical Latté

Tropical Latté designed and made by Gladys Schulz (102" x 85")

SKILL LEVEL: AVERAGE This colorful coffee theme quilt is a simple, but dramatic, presentation of the Tweaked Ohio Star blocks. Alternating the on-point blocks with plain dark blocks enlarges the quilt rapidly in this striking setting, and eliminates all the tricky bias-edged half and quarter blocks. The bright coffee cup fabric brings all the colors together and the pieced side triangles and scrappy border enhance the richness and tropical feel.

Quilt designer Gladys Schulz made this quilt as a wedding gift for a couple moving to the Nicaraguan coffee producing island of Ometepe. Bainbridge Island has a special sister relationship with Ometepe and the Bainbridge Island residents help sell Ometepe coffee, and assist in numerous community projects, such as providing clean water and building a health center, school and library.

MATERIALS FOR TROPICAL LATTÉ

Quilt size: 102" x 85"   Block size: 12"

Materials	Yards
Light fabric (blocks)	1½ (optional: use several fabrics)
Brightly colored fabric (blocks and side triangles)	1¾ (optional: use several fabrics)
Dark fabric (setting blocks and pieced side triangles)	2½
Light fabric (pieced side triangles and corners)	1
Pieced inner border	scraps/leftovers
Dark fabric (narrow middle border)	⅓
Coffee cup fabric (outer border)	2⅔
Dark fabric (binding)	¾
Batting 106" x 90"	
Backing 106" x 90"	

CUTTING FOR TROPICAL LATTÉ

Note: Use as many different light and brightly colored fabrics as desired. See page 66 for cutting single blocks.

Quilt parts	Cutting	Cutting
(12) pieced blocks	Light fabrics	Brightly colored fabrics
Star points	(24) 3¾" squares	(24) 3¾" squares
Half-square triangles	(24) 3½" squares	(24) 3½" squares
Center squares		(12) 3" squares
Framing strips	(96) 2¾" x 4¼"	
Triangles for framing strips		(96) 1¾" squares
Outer corners		(48) 2¾" squares

Setting blocks, pieced triangles and corners	
Dark setting blocks	(20) 12½" squares
Bright squares for pieced triangles	(14) 5½" squares
Dark strips for pieced triangles	(14) 2" x 5½", (14) 2" x 7"
Light triangles for pieced triangles	(7) 10½" squares cut diagonally both ways
Light corners	(2) 10" squares cut in half diagonally

Borders (Measure quilt before cutting exact length; adjust, if necessary.)	
Pieced inner border	(2) 2" x 85½"; (2) 2" x 71½"
Narrow middle border	(2) 1" x 88½"; (2) 1" x 72½"
Outer coffee cup border	(2) 7" x 89½"; (2) 7" x 85½" (cut lengthwise from fabric)

Constructing Tropical Latté

1 Construct the 12 Tweaked Ohio Star blocks (see pages 65-67).

2 Construct the pieced side triangles. Join one 5½" dark strip onto each of the colored squares. Press the seams toward the strips and add one 7" strip onto an adjacent side of each of the colored squares. Add the light triangles in the configuration shown in the picture.

3 Assemble the Tweaked Ohio Star blocks, dark setting blocks, pieced side triangles, and corners in diagonal rows (see page 27-28).

4 Piece the scrappy border from leftover fabrics in a variety of sizes and colors. Measure the center field and adjust the border lengths as necessary (see page 28). The center field should measure 85½" x 68½" before adding borders. Note that the plain setting squares float on the white background ¾" from the border and the dark strips around the colored squares in the side triangles come to a point right at the border (see photo).

5 Add the remaining borders, checking your measurements as you go.

6 Lay the quilt back flat, wrong side up, on a firm surface. Place the batting on top of the backing and smooth out. Layer the quilt top, right-side up, over the backing. Baste the layers and quilt as desired. Gladys designed an elegant curved quilting pattern for the pieced blocks and setting triangles. The rest of the quilt is quilted in a meandering stitch with variegated thread.

7 Add the binding.

Ohio Star Lattice - Star Struck

Star Struck pieced by the author, machine quilted by Wanda Rains (53" x 53")

SKILL LEVEL: AVERAGE Inserting a lattice (narrow strips that form a grid) into the Ohio Star block creates a new dimension. The hand-dyed fabrics provide subtle color variations and give the quilt a contemporary look. The prairie points add pizzazz and the Ohio Star theme is continued into the borders with the miniature blocks in the corners.

Star Struck has nine 12" Ohio Star lattice blocks, five with red/orange stars on light backgrounds and four with light stars on dark backgrounds. The four miniature corner blocks are 4¼". There are only five hand-dyed fabrics in the quilt, but because of the large variation in colors in each piece, the quilt looks much more complicated. The light stars and light backgrounds in the blocks are made from the same piece of fabric that includes a whole spectrum of colors from lemon yellow to light oranges and purples to soft blue. The double light and dark sashing helps to frame and highlight the blocks.

MATERIALS FOR STAR STRUCK

Quilt size: 53" x 53" Block sizes: 12" and 4¼"

Materials	Yards
Dark blue (blocks, cornerstones)	½
Multicolored light (blocks)	1
Light blue/green (blocks, sashing, inner border)	1
Rich blue/green (blocks, sashing, outer border)	1
Red/orange (blocks, cornerstones, prairie points)	1
Red/orange (binding)	½
Batting 56" x 56"	
Backing 56" x 56"	

CUTTING FOR STAR STRUCK

Quilt part	Fabric	Cutting
(5) 12" blocks - light background with red/orange stars		
Star points (quarter-square triangles)	Red/orange	(10) 4¾" squares
Star points (quarter-square triangles)	Multicolored light	(10) 4¾" squares
Center squares	Red/orange	(5) 4" squares
Corner squares	Multicolored light	(20) 4" squares
Lattice strips	Rich blue/green	(60) 1¼" x 4" (6 full-width 1¼" strips)
Cornerstones	Red/orange	(20) 1¼" squares
(4) 12" blocks - dark blue background with light stars		
Star points (quarter-square triangles)	Multicolored light	(8) 4¾" squares
Star points (quarter-square triangles)	Dark blue	(8) 4¾" squares
Center squares	Multicolored light	(4) 4" squares
Corner squares	Dark blue	(16) 4" squares
Lattice strips	Light blue/green	(48) 1¼" x 4" (5 full-width 1¼" strips)
Lattice cornerstones	Dark blue	(16) 1¾" squares
(4) 4¼" corner blocks - light background with red/orange stars		
Star points (quarter-square triangles)	Red/orange	(8) 2½" squares
Star points (quarter-square triangles)	Multicolored light	(8) 2½" squares
Center squares	Red/orange	(4) 1¾" squares
Corner squares	Multicolored light	(16) 1¾" squares
Lattice strips	Rich blue/green	(48) ¾" x 1¾" (1 full-width 1¾ strip)
Lattice cornerstones	Red/orange	(16) ¾" squares

CUTTING FOR STAR STRUCK (CONTINUED)

Quilt part	Fabric	Cutting
Sashing, cornerstones, and borders		
Sashing	Light blue/green	(9) full-width 1½" strips
Sashing	Rich blue/green	(9) full-width 1½" strips
Cornerstones	Red/orange	(8) 2½" squares
Cornerstones	Dark blue	(8) 2½" squares
Sashing for outer edges of corners	Rich blue/green	(8) 1½" x 4¾" (from 1 full-width 1½" strip)
Outer side rectangles	Dark blue	(8) 2½" x 1½"
Outer corner squares	Red	(4) 1½" squares
Inner border strips	Light blue/green	(4) 2" x 40½"
Outer border strips	Rich blue/green	(4) 4¼" x 40½"
Prairie points	Red	(your choice) 2½" to 4" squares

Constructing Star Struck

1 Cut and piece each set of Ohio Star lattice blocks in turn. Make the quarter-square triangle units for the star points (see page 17); trim to 4" for the 12" blocks and 1¼" for the 4¼" blocks. Lay out the block components including the lattice and cornerstones; join them in rows. Press all seams toward the lattice, i.e., away from the block pieces and cornerstones. Assemble the rows to complete the blocks (see page 20).

2 Strip-piece the nine full-width strips of light blue/green and rich blue/green. Counter-cut the pieced strips (24) 12½" and (8) 4¾" for the double sashing.

3 Assemble the center field of the quilt from the large blocks, 12½" double sashing strips and 2½" cornerstones (see pages 25-27).

4 Lay out the center field with the border pieces, corner blocks and prairie points. Follow the pieceing instructions carefully and refer to the illustration.

5 Join the inner and outer long border strips, inserting prairie points as desired (see page 22).

6 Attach the dark blue rectangles to the 4¾" double sashing strips. Join these sections onto each end of the long border strips inserting prairie points (see page 22). Make sure the rectangles are on the outer edges.

7 Attach the (8) 1½" x 4¾" rich blue/green sashing strips and four red cornerstones onto the outer edges of the miniature Ohio Star blocks.

8 Attach the side borders to the center field of the quilt. Sew the miniature Ohio Star blocks onto each end of the top and bottom borders, being careful to orient them correctly. Sew to the top and bottom of the quilt.

9 Lay the quilt back flat, wrong side up, on a firm surface. Place the batting on top of the backing and smooth out. Layer the quilt top, right-side up, over the backing. Baste the layers and quilt as desired. Quilter Wanda Rains quilted in the ditch along all the seams and added diagonal lines across the blocks extending into the border and sashing. The zigzags in the border complement the prairie points.

10 Add the binding.

CORNER SECTIONS OF STAR STRUCK

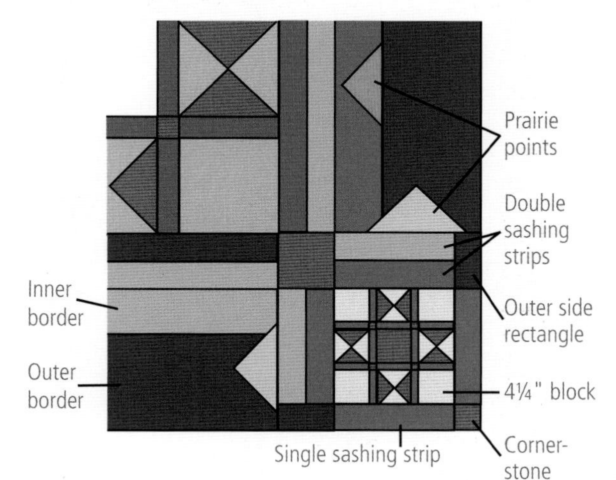

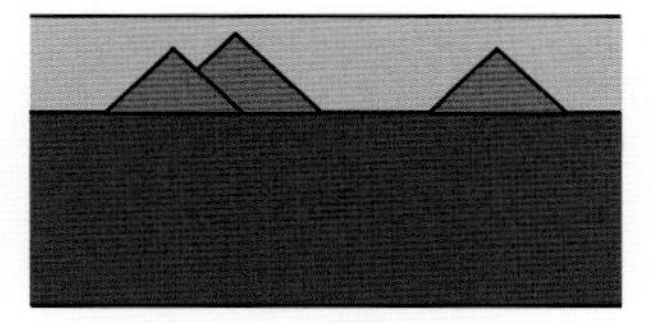

Join inner and outer border strips, inserting prairie points as desired.

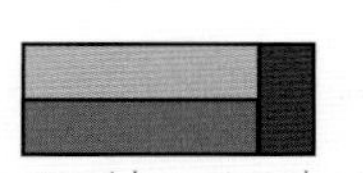

Add outer side rectangles to 4¾" double sashing strips.

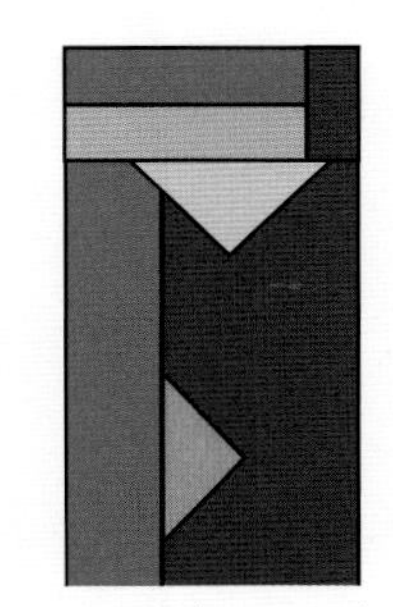

Attach sashing strips with rectangle onto each end of the long double border, inserting prairie points.

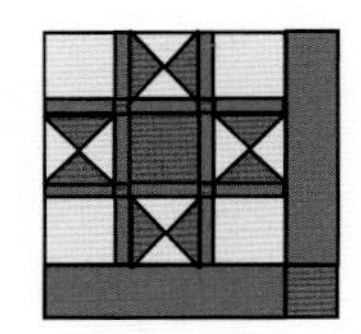

Attach single sashing strips and corner-stones to two sides of the 4¼" blocks.

More Lattice Quilts

Take the lattice concept a step further and insert a lattice (narrow strips that form a grid) into any nine-patch block. The lattice coloration can create interesting secondary patterns across the block boundaries, providing more design possibilities.

For a very simple project, use the basic nine-patch. Cut nine 4" squares from each of nine fabrics. Arrange the 81 squares into nine nine-patches and insert the same size of lattice as used for the Ohio Star project. Change the color and size of the lattice and sashing strips between the blocks for more variations.

In the samples illustrated here, I've added half-square triangles and rectangles to make the Shoofly and Monkey Wrench patterns — both nine-patch blocks — and inserted lattices. Notice how the colors in Shoofly Lattice extend across adjacent blocks to generate a secondary pattern. In the Monkey Wrench, I've pieced parts of the sashing creating additional patterns. Once again, the prairie points provide extra interest.

Caution, Zebra Crossing! made by the author (53" x 53")
Photo by Mark Frey

Shoofly Lattice made by the author (56½" x 56½")

There is no reason why the lattice idea should be confined to nine-patches. Use it in four-patches or in any other blocks. Experiment and create your own unique patterns.

1920s Amish Bear's Paw. From the collection of Joe and Mary Koval

CHAPTER FIVE

Bear's Paw

The Bear's Paw is one of my favorite blocks. I find the symmetry pleasing and like the way the four sections of the block are linked by the small central square. (In fact, the completion of my 13-block Bear's Paw sampler set me on this book-writing path.) It seemed to me that the large squares in the block were begging for more intricacy, so I substituted them with several mini-blocks to generate the new blocks presented in the next projects.

Hydrangea Garden made by Barbara Michael (58¾" x 58¾")
Photo by Mark Frey

One approach to twisting the original pattern is to choose unusual or non-traditional colors and settings. Val Martinson's quilt is a beautiful illustration. The vibrant blocks in autumnal shades with a creative border setting give this traditional quilt a contemporary flavor. Some of the bears recede into the background and others pop right out. Her beautiful hand quilting softens and enhances the design.

I made Round and Round the Seasons like a Teddy Bear for a local guild challenge. The challenge was to design a quilt for all seasons, so I pieced the central bear using a pattern by Margaret Rolfe and surrounded it with Bear's Paw blocks that change throughout the year. Winter begins the cycle with snowflakes and Christmas trees, followed clockwise by pussy willows, daffodils, irises, summer flowers, fall leaves, and a carved Halloween pumpkin and Thanksgiving food.

25 Bears Hiding in the Woods made by Valerie Martinson (76" x 76")
Photo by Mark Frey

Round and Round the Seasons like a Teddy Bear made by the author (45" x 45")
Photo by Mark Frey

Constructing the Bear's Paw Blocks

Block variations of the Bear's Paw are made by subdividing the four large squares in the block into pieced mini-blocks such as Bowties, Pinwheels, and Sawtooth Stars. In all the blocks, the half-square triangle bear claws and the center square are retained so that they are instantly recognizable as belonging to the Bear's Paw family. This creates unity in sampler quilts that combine several different blocks and maintains the integrity of pattern.

The Bear's Paw block size is 12¼" for all the quilt patterns provided, so the cutting sizes for the block components are consistent throughout. The only variable is in the four large squares subdivided into the mini-blocks, except in one pattern where the background within the block is also divided to create an Ohio Star in the center. Use the cutting sizes for the traditional Bear's Paw block, substituting the large squares with pieced mini-blocks as instructed for each pattern. In all cases, piece the mini-blocks first, and then follow the general piecing directions for the traditional Bear's Paw as given on page 94.

Traditional Bear's Paw Block

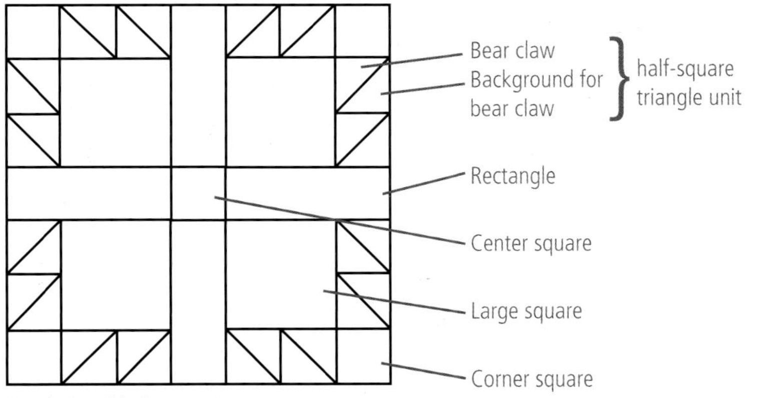

Bear's Paw block components

Dark Bear's Paw on light background

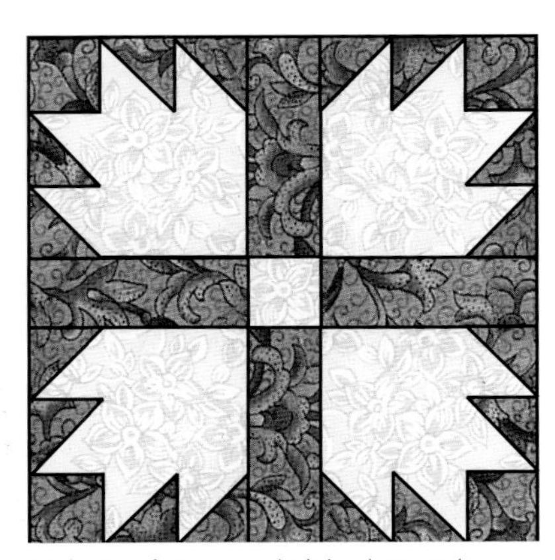

Light Bear's Paw on dark background

CUTTING FOR ONE BLOCK

Block size - 12¼"

Note: Use as many different background and contrast fabrics as desired.

Block part	Background fabric	Contrast fabric
Bear claws (half-square triangles)	(8) 2¾" squares	(8) 2¾" squares
Large squares		(4) 4" squares
Center square		(1) 2¼" square
Rectangles	(4) 2¼" x 5¾"	
Corner squares	(4) 2¼" squares	

1 Construct the half-square triangle bear claws (see page 16). Trim to 2¼".

2 Lay out the block components to ensure the correct orientation of the bear claws.

3 Construct the corner units consisting of the large square (or mini-block for the pattern variations), four half-square triangle units, and a corner square. Join the bear claws in pairs, and then add the corner squares to four of them. Press the seams toward the dark triangles. Sew the pairs without corner squares onto the large squares; press the seams toward the triangles. Add the pairs with corner squares; press the seams toward the triangles.

4 Assemble the block components in rows; press the seams toward the background rectangles. Stitch the three rows together to complete the block; press the seams toward the background rectangles. Refer to the illustrations for help.

CONSTRUCTION OF BEAR'S PAW BLOCK

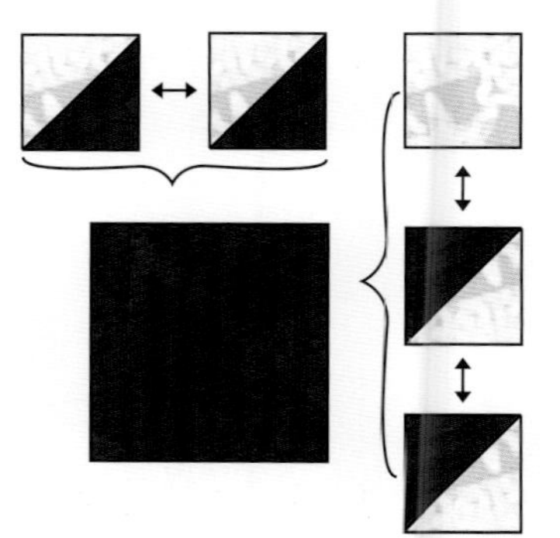

Piecing of corner sections of Bear's Paw block

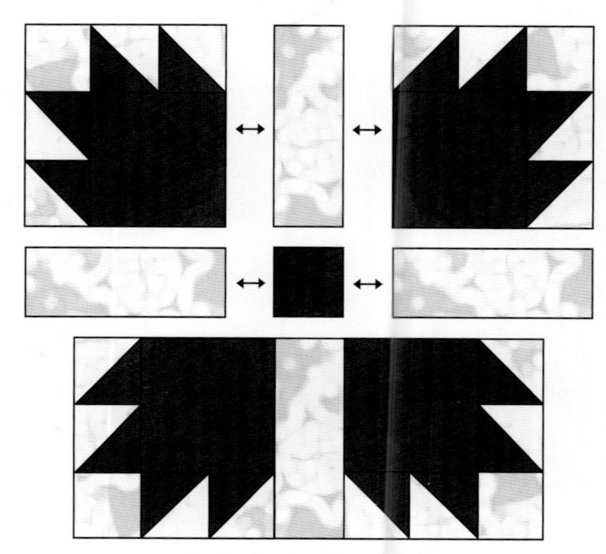

Piecing for Bear's Paw block

Wrong side of Bear's Paw block; press seams as shown.

CUTTING FOR MULTIPLE BLOCKS

Note: Use table for cutting all block components except large squares or mini-blocks.
Asterisked figures are number of full-width 42" strips required to yield pieces.

Block part	Size	6-blocks	9-blocks	13-blocks
Background bear claws	2¾" squares	48 *4	72 *5	104 *7
Contrast bear claws	2¾" squares	48 *4	72 *5	104 *7
Contrast center square	2¼" squares	6 *1	9 *1	13 *1
Background rectangles	2¼" x 5¾"	24 *4 @ 2¼"	36 *6 @ 2¼"	52 *8 @ 2¼"
Background corner squares	2¼" squares	24 *2	36 *2	52 *3

Bear's Paw Variations

The samples show some of the block variations used in the quilts. Changing the background, value placements and orientation of the mini-blocks opens up numerous possibilities. Feel free to improvise and create your own unique blocks.

Winter Garden

Hydrangea Garden

SPOOLS

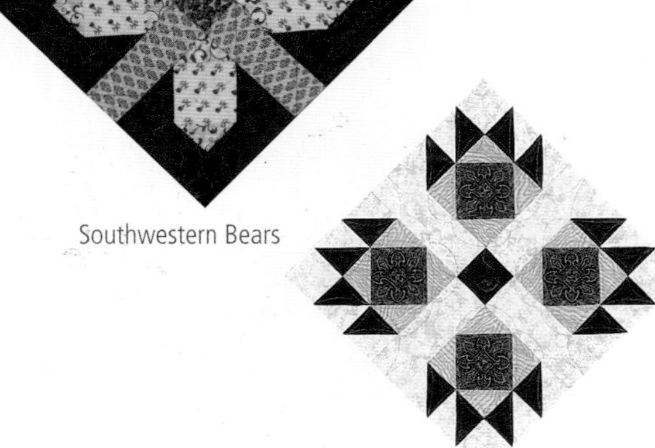

Southwestern Bears

Winter Garden

SQUARE-ON-POINT

Pacific Northwest Bears

Southwestern Bears

PINWHEELS

Winter Garden

Royal Bears

BOWTIES

Winter Garden

Royal Bears

BIRDS OF THE AIR

Winter Garden

The Bears Come Out at Night

SAWTOOTH STARS

Winter Garden

Pacific Northwest Bears

PUSS-IN-THE-CORNER

Pacific Northwest Bears

Hydrangea Garden

16-PATCH

Marcia's Sampler

Royal Bears

WEDGES

Menopausal Bears

Menopausal Bears

Tuscany Bears

MIX AND MATCH THE MINI-BLOCKS

Choose your favorite blocks for your quilt. Make all the blocks from the same pattern, make two of each, or any combination that you fancy. Follow the general directions for the traditional Bear's Paw, substituting the four large squares for four mini-blocks.

CUTTING AND PIECING THE MINI-BLOCKS FOR ONE BLOCK

Note: Mini-block size is 4" unfinished, four mini-blocks in each block. Instructions for half-square triangles are on page 16 and for corner-square triangles on page 15. Optional: Use more than two fabrics.

Mini-block	Fabric A	Fabric B	Piecing Notes
Square-on-point	(4) 4" square	(16) 2¼" squares	Fabric A may be fussy-cut for motifs. Use corner-square triangle method.
Bowties	(8) 2¼" squares (8) 1¼" squares	(8) 2¼" squares	Make small triangles for Bowties using corner-square triangle method. Bowtie instructions on page 18.
Spools	(8) 2¼" squares (4) 2¾" squares	(4) 2¾" squares	Use 2¾" squares to make (8) half-square triangles. Trim to 2¼". Piece with other 2¼" squares.
Pinwheels	(8) 2¾" squares	(8) 2¾" squares	Make half-square triangles; trim to 2¼". Assemble pinwheels. Press final seams open.
Birds of the Air	(4) 2¼" squares (2) 4⅜" squares cut in half diagonally	(4) 2⅝" squares cut in half diagonally.	Attach small triangles to small squares to make large triangles. Join to large triangles.
Sawtooth Stars	(4) 2¼" squares (32) 1⅜" squares	(16) 1⅜" squares (16) 2¼" x 1⅜"	Use corner-square triangle method to add (2) star points to each rectangle. Sawtooth Star instructions on page 19.
Puss-in-the-corner	(4) 2¼" squares (2) 1⅜" x 15"	(1) 2¼" x 15" (8) 2¼" x 1⅜"	Stitch 15" strips, - Fabrics ABA and press seams toward dark. Counter-cut into (8) 1⅜". Join (8) B rectangles to opposite sides of 2¼" squares. Add pieced sections to other sides.
16-patch	(2) 1⅜" x 26"	(2) 1⅜" x 26"	Strip-piece fabrics ABAB. Press all seams in one direction. Counter-cut (16) 1⅜" and join into 16-patches.
Wedges	(4) 4" squares	(8) 2¼" x 4" (4) 2¼" squares	Wedges instructions on pages 20-21.

Mix and Match: Combine any four mini-blocks to make the block. (See sample projects on pages 118-122.)

Ohio Star Center

Use this attractive setting with any of the mini-blocks to make more Bear's Paw blocks.

CUTTING AND PIECING FOR ONE BLOCK WITH OHIO STAR CENTER

Note: Block size is 12¼". Substitute background (4) 2¼" x 5¾" rectangles as follows:

Part	Background	Contrast
Rectangles	(4) 2¼" x 4"	
Quarter-square triangle units	(2) 3" squares	(2) 3" squares

Construct quarter-square triangle units (see page 17); trim to 2¼". Join one unit to each rectangle.

Table Runner

SKILL LEVEL: AVERAGE Select any three blocks for this decorative table runner. This is an excellent way to practice the block before moving on to a more challenging quilt top. In the sample, designer Joanne Bennett has oriented the Bowtie mini-blocks in different ways with Ohio Star centers and used colored rectangles in the blocks.

Table runners made by Joanne Bennett (21¾" x 48¼")

MATERIALS FOR THREE-BLOCK TABLE RUNNER

Table runner size: 21¾" x 48¼" Block size: 12¼"

Materials	Yards
Light background (blocks)	½
Background (rectangles in blocks)	¼
Red or green (bear claws)	¼
Red or green Bowties (mini-blocks)	¼
Sashing	¼
Border and binding	¾
Batting 24" x 50"	
Backing 24" x 50"	

Constructing the Table Runner

1 Use the cutting and piecing directions to make three Bear's Paw blocks of your choice (see pages 93-95, 97-99).

2 Cut four 1½" x 12¾" and two 1½" x 41¼" sashing strips. Assemble with the blocks, making a row of short strips and blocks, and then adding the long strips to the top and bottom. Press the seams toward the sashing strips.

3 Cut two 4" x 41¼" and two 4" x 14¾" borders. Sew the two long borders first and then add the short ones on each end. Press the seams toward the borders.

4 Lay the quilt back flat, wrong side up, on a firm surface. Place the batting on top of the backing and smooth out. Layer the quilt top, right-side up, over the backing. Baste the layers and quilt as desired. Joanne quilted in the ditch around all the Bear's Paw blocks and also ¼" inside every Bowtie within the blocks. On one table runner she quilted with a meandering stitch in the border and on the other she stitched a cable.

5 Add the binding.

Six-Block Samplers

Pacific Northwest Bears, pieced and hand quilted by author (66½" x 54¼")

Royal Bears, pieced by author, machine quilted by Wanda Rains (66½" x 54¼")

SKILL LEVEL: AVERAGE Choose six of your favorite Bear's Paw blocks to create an attractive sampler quilt. The fabric value placement within the blocks, setting squares and triangles will dramatically affect the look of your quilt. For example, Pacific Northwest Bears, is soft and mellow and enhanced by the hand quilting, which is beautifully displayed in the alternating light blocks. In contrast, Royal Bears is rich and majestic with darker rectangles within the blocks and heavily saturated blue setting squares and triangles.

MATERIALS FOR PACIFIC NORTHWEST BEARS

Quilt size: 66½" x 54¼"   Block size: 12¼"

Materials	Yards
Light (blocks, setting squares and triangles)	2
Dark green (blocks)	¼
Dark brown (blocks)	¼
Green (mini-blocks, outer border)	1¾
Beige flower (middle border)	¾
Brown (mini-blocks, inner border)	¾
Brown (binding)	⅔
Batting 70" x 58"	
Backing 70" x 58"	

MATERIALS FOR ROYAL BEARS

Quilt size: 66½" x 54¼"   Block size: 12¼"

Materials	Yards
Light (blocks, middle border)	1¾
Multi (mini-blocks, outer border)	1¾
Red (blocks, inner border)	¾
Blue (blocks)	⅓
Blue/yellow print (setting squares and triangles)	1
Blue/yellow print (binding)	⅔
Batting 70" x 58"	
Backing 70" x 58"	

Constructing the six-block sampler

1 Cut two 5½" x 62" and two 4" x 62" strips from the outer border fabric before cutting the mini-blocks. These strips will be trimmed to their precise length just before attaching to the quilt top

2 Make six Bear's Paw blocks of your choice (see pages 93-95, 97-99).

3 Cut the two plain setting blocks 12¾" square. To make the setting triangles, cut a 20" full-width piece of fabric. From this, cut two 20" squares. Divide the squares diagonally into quarters to yield eight triangles. Cut two of these triangles in half to make the four corner triangles. Refer to the diagram for help.

CUT THE SETTING AND CORNER TRIANGLES.

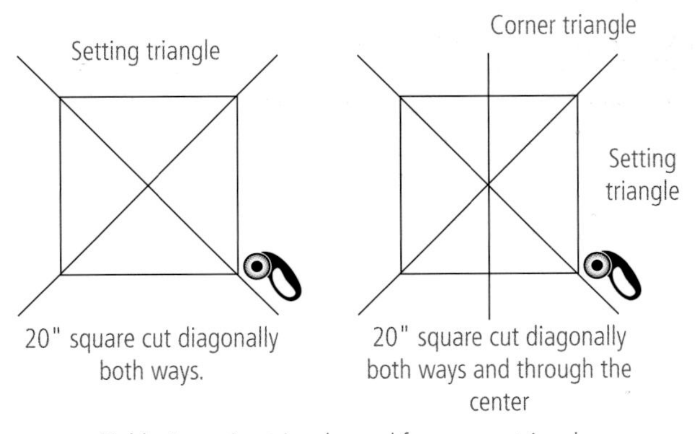

Yields six setting triangles and four corner triangles

4 Assemble the blocks with the setting triangles and squares in diagonal rows (see pages 27-28). Note that the side and corner triangles are larger than necessary. Press the seams away from the pieced blocks. Join the rows to complete the quilt center. Trim away the excess around the edges being careful to leave the ¼" seam allowance. Make sure that the corners remain square (see page 28).

5 Attach the borders to the sides of the quilt, then the top and bottom (see page 28). Note that the middle and outer borders are wider on the sides than at the top and bottom. Join strips for the inner and middle borders to attain the required lengths (see page 28). Press all border seams away from the center of the quilt.

CUTTING OF BORDER STRIPS

Check the size of the center field and adjust the borders, if necessary (see page 28).

Border	Sides	Top and Bottom
Inner border	(2) 2" x 52¾"	(2) 2" x 38¼"
Middle border	(2) 3½" x 55¾"	(2) 2½" x 44¼"
Outer border	(2) 5½" x 59¾"	(2) 4" x 54¼"

6 Lay the quilt back flat, wrong side up, on a firm surface. Place the batting on top of the backing and smooth out. Layer the quilt top, right-side up, over the backing. Baste the layers and quilt as desired. Pacific Northwest Bears is hand-quilted in the ditch around the pieced blocks and diagonally across the mini-blocks. More Bear's Paws were added in the setting squares and triangles as well as leaves; diagonal lines were stitched in the borders.

7 Add the binding.

A sample of Pacific Northwest Bears hand quilting

Quilter Wanda Rains custom quilted Royal Bears along with quilting in the ditch along all seamlines. The sample features leafy vines, tendrils and cables in the borders and the setting blocks and triangles are filled with a deliciously intricate pattern of leaves, berries, and hearts.

The Bears Come Out at Night

The Bears Come Out at Night, made by the author (55" x 37")

SKILL LEVEL: CHALLENGING What a difference when the Bear's Paw blocks are presented on a black background. The mini-block Sawtooth Stars in jewel tones stand out like little gems and the Ohio Stars in the setting squares and triangles make this quilt sparkle. I used the same six-block on-point format as for the six-block sampler quilts.

MATERIALS FOR THE BEARS COME OUT AT NIGHT

Quilt size: 55" x 37"
Block sizes: 12¼, 7½"; 4½"; 3"

Materials	Yards
Mini-block Sawtooth Stars (24 fabrics)	⅛ of each
Black (background)	2½
Gold (Ohio Stars, bear claws)	¾
Gold (binding)	½
Backing 59" x 42"	
Batting 59" x 42"	

Constructing The Bears Come Out at Night

1 Make six Sawtooth Star Bear's Paw blocks (see pages 93-95, 98). The sample quilt features a different fabric for each of the 24 stars. Make individual mini-blocks (see page 98). Cut the star fabric for four stars at a time, layering the four fabrics and cutting a rectangle 3" x 8¼". From this rectangle, cut the 2¼" square, then two strips of 1⅜" to yield the eight 1⅜" squares. For the background fabric for all 24 stars, you'll need 96 1⅜" squares (four full-width 1⅜" strips) and 96 rectangles 2¼" x 1⅜" (four full-width 2¼" strips). For the remaining block components, refer to cutting multiple blocks, page 95. Use any combination of fabrics to sprinkle colored stars across the quilt top.

2 Construct the 7½", 4½" and 3" Ohio Star blocks (see page 20). Add the strips and triangles to the blocks to complete them for setting with the Sawtooth Star Bear's Paw blocks (see page 108). The 7½" blocks are framed on all four sides.

CUTTING AND INSTRUCTIONS FOR OHIO STAR SETTING BLOCKS

Block part	Cutting	Piecing notes
(2) setting squares with 7½" Ohio Star blocks		
Background star points (quarter-square triangles)	(4) 3¾" squares	Construct quarter-square triangle units; trim to 3" (see page 17).
Gold star points (quarter-square triangles)	(4) 3¾" squares	
Gold star center squares	(2) 3" squares	Assemble Ohio Star blocks (see page 20).
Background (corners)	(8) 3" squares	
Background (framing strips)	(2) 3" x 8", (2) 3" x 13"	Attach to Ohio stars; trim blocks to 12¾" (approximately ⅛" off each side).
(6) setting side triangles with 4½" Ohio Star blocks		
Background star points (quarter-square triangles)	(12) 2¾" squares	Construct quarter-square triangle units; trim to 2" (page 17).
Gold star points (quarter-square triangles)	(12) 2¾" squares	
Gold star center squares	(6) 2" squares	Assemble Ohio Star blocks (page 20).
Background (corners)	(24) 2" squares	
Background (additional triangles)	(3) 8½" squares cut diagonally both ways	
Background (framing strips)	(5) full-width 2½" strips	See notes below.
(4) setting corner triangles with 3" Ohio Star blocks		
Background star points (quarter-square triangles)	(8) 2¼" squares	
Gold star points (quarter-square triangles)	(8) 2¼" squares	Construct quarter-square triangle units; trim to 1½" (see page 17).
Gold star center squares	(4) 1½" squares	Assemble Ohio Star blocks (see page 20).
Background (corners)	(16) 1½" squares	
Background (additional triangles)	(2) 6½" squares cut diagonally both ways.	
Background (additional triangles)	(2) 4¼" squares cut diagonally in half.	
Background (framing strips)	(2) full-width 2¾" strips	See notes below.

For the six setting side triangles, join the additional background triangles onto two adjacent sides of the 4½" Ohio Stars to make a large triangle. The Ohio Star block is on-point. Add the strips to the remaining two short sides of the triangle to complete. Assembly-line piece these strips, leaving a gap of 3" between the end of one triangle and the start of the next to allow for the edges to be cut at a 45-degree angle.

STEP-BY-STEP CONSTRUCTION OF SETTING TRIANGLES

Add triangles.

Add strips and trim along dotted line at 45-degree angle in line with the edge of the triangle.

Completed setting triangle

For the four corner triangles, join two triangles (from 6½" squares) onto opposite sides of each 3" Ohio Star; add one triangle (from 4½" squares) onto the corner. Sew the strip to the long edge allowing enough at each end for the 45-degree angle.

STEP-BY-STEP CONSTRUCTION OF CORNER TRIANGLES

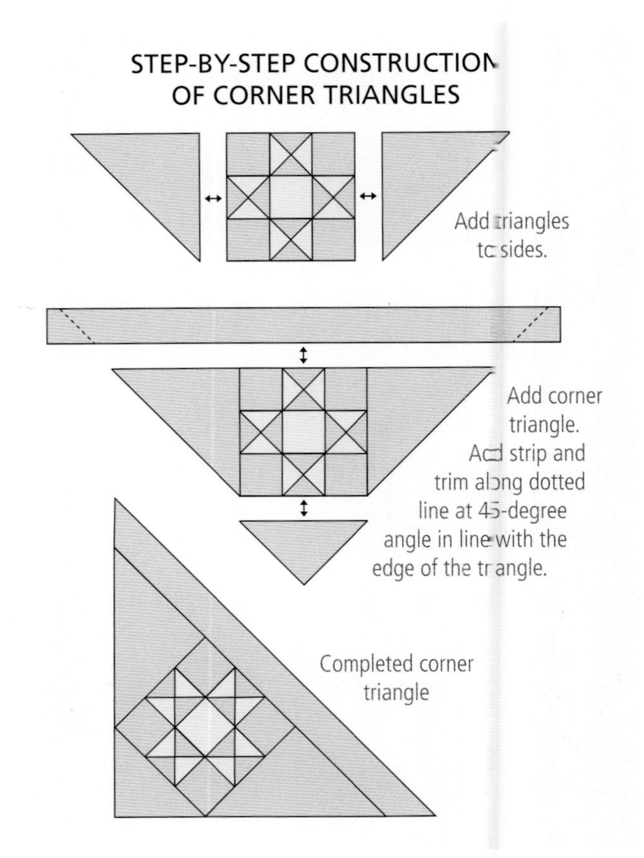

3 Assemble the blocks with the setting triangles, squares and corners in diagonal rows and trim to leave ¼" seam allowance (see pages 27-28). There will be some overlap at the edges of the setting triangles, because the Ohio Stars float on the background and the setting triangles are larger than half of a Bear's Paw block. Simply keep the seams straight and square with the Sawtooth Star Bear's Paw blocks and trim off the excess triangles from the seam allowances.

4 Lay the quilt back flat, wrong side up, on a firm surface. Place the batting on top of the backing and smooth out. Layer the quilt top, right-side up, over the backing. Baste the layers and quilt as desired. The sample was machine quilted around the blocks in black thread to stabilize the quilt and then I had fun with the gold thread. The serpentine stitches radiate from the Ohio Stars and echo quilting is stitched ½" beyond the outline of the large stars and Bear's Paws. The finishing touch was free-motion machine quilting five-pointed stars in the centers of each of the colored Sawtooth Star mini-blocks.

5 Add the binding

Hydrangea Garden

Hydrangea Garden made by Barbara Michael (58¾" x 58¾"). Photo by Mark Frey

SKILL LEVEL: AVERAGE Pick and choose nine Bear's Paw blocks to make a lap quilt or wall hanging with a pretty triple sashing and nine-patches. Once the blocks are pieced, the top goes together quickly and easily.

MATERIALS FOR HYDRANGEA GARDEN

Quilt size: 58¾" x 58¾"   Block size: 12¼"

Materials	Yards
Light (blocks, inner border)	2
Multi hydrangea (mini-blocks, outer border)	1½
Green hydrangea (mini-blocks, sashing, nine-patches)	1
Dark blue (blocks)	½
Burgundy (mini-blocks)	¼
Bright blue (mini-blocks)	¼
Medium blue calico print (mini-blocks)	¼
Light calico print (mini-blocks)	¼
Purple floral (sashing, nine-patches, border corners)	1¼
Purple floral (binding)	⅔
Backing 63" x 63"	
Batting 63" x 63"	

Constructing Hydrangea Garden

1 Cut four 53" x 4½" strips for the outer border before cutting pieces for the mini-blocks. These strips will be trimmed to the precise length before attaching to the quilt top.

2 Make nine Bear's Paw blocks of your choice (see pages 93-95, 97-99).

CUTTING FOR SASHING, NINE-PATCHES AND BORDERS

Note: Check the size of your center field and adjust the borders, if necessary.

Quilt part	Fabric	Cutting
Sashing strips	Green hydrangea	(8) full-width 1½" strips
Sashing strips	Purple floral	(16) full-width 1½" strips
Nine-patches	Green hydrangea	(5) full-width 1½" strips
Nine-patches	Purple floral	(4) full-width 1½" strips
Inner border	Light	(5) full width 1½" strips to make (4) 1½" x 49¼"
Inner border corners	Purple floral	(4) 1½" squares
Outer border	Multi hydrangea	(4) 4½" x 51¼" (trim previously cut strips)
Outer border corners	Purple floral	(4) 4½" squares

3 Strip-piece the sashing strips: purple, green, purple. Counter-cut (24) 12¾" triple-sashing strips.

4 Strip-piece the 16 nine-patches for the cornerstones (see page 15). Sew two sets of green, purple, green, and one set of purple, green, purple. Press the seams toward the purple. Counter-cut (32) 1½" green, purple, green and (16) 1½" purple, green, purple. Complete the 16 nine-patches.

5 Assemble the center field of the quilt from the blocks, triple-sashing strips and nine-patches (see page 25-27).

6 The center field should measure 49¼" x 49¼". Check yours and make adjustments to the border strips, if necessary. Attach the inner border with corners, then the outer border with corners to the quilt top (see page 28).

7 Lay the quilt back flat, wrong side up, on a firm surface. Place the batting on top of the backing and smooth out. Layer the quilt top, right-side up, over the backing. Baste the layers and quilt as desired. Quilt designer Barbara Michael machine quilted a small serpentine stitch outlining the sashing strips and mini-blocks and hand quilted following the geometric shapes of the bear claws and within the mini-blocks. She quilted hearts in the four large corner squares.

8 Add the binding.

Note the two different settings of the Birds of the Air mini-blocks and the use of three colors in the Bowtie mini-blocks.

Hydrangea Garden
Photo by Mark Frey

Winter Garden

Winter Garden pieced by the author, machine quilted by Wanda Rains (86" x 86")

SKILL LEVEL: CHALLENGING This intricate 13-block Bear's Paw sampler makes a gorgeous queen-sized bed-quilt. It's the most challenging and time-consuming project in the book, but well worth the effort if you are prepared to give it a go. The patterns in the borders and setting triangles may be easily simplified and there are many opportunities for improvising. The three examples show how color choices and value placements can produce dramatically differing quilts.

MATERIALS FOR WINTER GARDEN

Quilt size: 86" x 86" Block size: 12¼"

Materials	Yards
Assorted fabrics (mini-blocks)	scraps, less than ¼
Blue (blocks)	½
Light background (blocks, nine-patches, setting triangles, pieced border)	2½
Red (blocks, sashing, nine-patches, pieced border)	1½
Brown (blocks, sashing, nine-patches)	1
Holly (sashing, nine-patches)	½
Beige patterned (sashing)	¾
Gold (setting triangles, borders)	1
Black (setting triangles, pieced and outer borders)	4
Binding	¾
Batting 90" x 90"	
Backing 90" x 90"	

Marcia's Sampler made by Marcia Barrett (84" x 84")
Photo by Mark Frey

Constructing Winter Garden

Begin by reading these instructions and making notes so that you understand which of your fabrics correspond to the fabrics used in the sample. This is a complex pattern, but if you remain well organized and systematic in your approach, you can complete the project. Taking a step-by-step approach and dealing with each component before moving on to the next is recommended.

1 Make 13 Bear's Paw blocks of your choice (see pages 93-95, 97-99).

2 Strip-piece the 36 sashing strips and the 12 nine-patch cornerstones.

CUTTING FOR TRIPLE SASHING AND NINE-PATCHES

Fabric	Cutting
Red set of triple sashing: strip-piece and counter-cut (16) 12¾"	
Red	(6) full-width 1½" strips
Beige	(12) full-width 1½" strips

Brown set of triple sashing: strip-piece and counter-cut (20) 12¾"	
Holly	(7) full-width 1½" strips
Brown	(14) full-width 1½" strips

Nine-patches: counter-cut strip sets 1½" and complete blocks (see page 15) (See photos and illustration for further details.)	
Light background	(3) full width 1½" strips
Red	(1) full width 1½" strip
Holly	(1) full width 1½" strip
Holly	(8) 1½" x 3½" from the full-width strip
Holly	(1) 2½" x 8"

3 Construct the eight pieced setting triangles. For plain triangles (like Marcia's Sampler) cut two 18⅝" squares diagonally both ways to yield eight triangles with the long edges on the straight-of-grain. For the eight pieced setting triangles like those in Winter Garden, use partial Bear's Paw blocks with sashing and triangles. Construct the partial Bear's Paw blocks; add the sashing strips with triangular cornerstones, then large triangles.

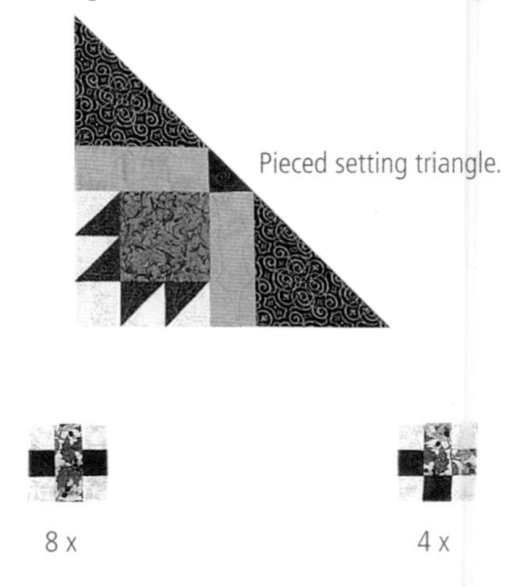
Pieced setting triangle.

8 x   4 x

NINE-PATCHES IN WINTER GARDEN AND THE THREE-SQUARE UNITS REQUIRED TO MAKE THEM

8 x

4 x

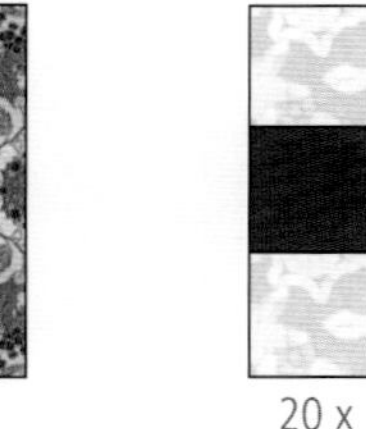
8 x 1½" x 3½" strip

20 x

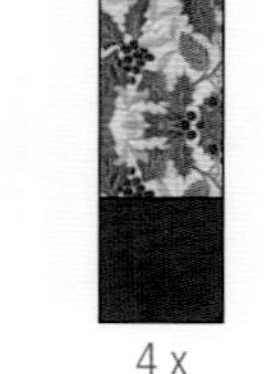
4 x Use the 2½" x 8" strip

4 x

CUTTING FOR PIECED SETTING TRIANGLES AND CORNERS

Piece	Fabric	Size
Pieced setting triangles		
Bear claws (half-square triangles)	Blue	(16) 2¾" squares
Bear claws (half-square triangles)	Light background	(16) 2¾" squares
Corner squares	Light background	(8) 2¼" squares
Large squares	Blue patterned	(8) 4" squares
Sashing	Gold	(16) 2¼" x 5¾"
Triangular cornerstones	Red	(2) 3¾" squares cut diagonally both ways
Large triangles	Black	(4) 8¾" squares cut diagonally both ways
Corners		
Corner triangles	Black	(2) 9½" squares cut in half diagonally

4 Lay out the blocks, sashing strips, nine-patches, pieced setting triangles and corners in the desired configuration. Assemble in diagonal rows to complete the center field (see pages 25-28). Carefully trim away any excess on the outer edges so that you have an accurate ¼" seam allowance and the quilt top is square.

5 Add the borders of your choice. Note: Remember the importance of measuring accurately across the center of the quilt to calculate the precise size of the border strips (see page 28). The pieced borders are the most challenging part of making this quilt. Any discrepancies in the seam allowances adds up quickly when it's repeated so many times.

Winter Garden and Southwest Bears have on-point large and small squares. Heather Coats avoided the problem of making the pieced border fit exactly on Southwestern Bears by stopping it before the corners and adding solid pieces to each end (see photo page 117). The size of the solid pieces easily can be adjusted to make the border fit exactly.

Winter Garden has 19 units of squares on each side plus corners that fit precisely. Adjust the pattern slightly, if there's a discrepancy. Center it on the side, and make the changes at each end so that the pattern remains symmetrical. If this seems too challenging, stop the pieced border design short of the ends; or use a plain border.

For Winter Garden, attach the inner gold borders (see page 28). Measure across the center of the quilt, cut two of the strips the same length and join them to the sides of the quilt. Measure again to include the two side strips, cut the top and bottom strips the same length and sew to the quilt. Alternatively, miter with the second pieced border (see pages 23-24).

Make and attach the pieced border with 19 units on each side (see pages 23-24).

Join the remaining four narrow gold strips to the four wide black outer border strips. Carefully measure the quilt across the center in both directions, it should be square. Complete the quilt top by adding these borders and mitering the corners (see page 28).

6 Lay the quilt back flat, wrong side up, on a firm surface. Place the batting on top of the backing and smooth out. Layer the quilt top, right-side up, over the backing. Baste the layers and quilt as desired. Quilter Wanda Rains quilted in the ditch around all the blocks and along the sashing strips. The bear claws have curved stitching lines just inside the triangles and the sashing within the blocks has curves that look like holly leaves. Quilting within the mini-blocks varies for each type and there is a curlicue in the central square of each block. The curlicues are repeated in the small squares of the pieced border; the outer border has diagonal straight lines.

7 Add the binding.

Squares on-point border
Winter Garden

CUTTING AND NOTES FOR BORDERS FOR WINTER GARDEN

Notes: The asterisked figures are numbers of full-width 42" strips required to yield pieces.
Measure the center field after adding each border to determine the precise size of the next border.
Instructions for constructing the second pieced border are on pages 23-24.

Border part	Fabric	Cutting	Notes
First and third borders	Gold	(16) full-width 1½" strips	Join in pairs and trim to precise length.
Pieced second border	Black	(80) 3" squares *7	
Pieced second border	Red	(40) 3½" squares *4	These will be cut into four after piecing.
Pieced second border	Light	(80) 3½" squares *8	Cut in half diagonally.
Pieced second border	Light	(2) 3" squares	Cut in half diagonally for corners
Outer border	Black	(4) 5½" x 88"	Join with third gold border and miter

Southwestern Bears made by Heather Coats (74" x 74")
Photo by Mark Frey

Mix and Match - Tuscany Bears

Tuscany Bears pieced by the author, machine quilted by Wanda Rains (51" x 51")

SKILL LEVEL: CHALLENGING Choose your favorite mini-blocks to create your own unique Bear's Paw blocks. Instead of making all four the same in one block, play around with the placement. Arrange them any way you want and use as many different fabrics as you like. The challenge here is to maintain balance in the design through appropriate choices of fabric; being careful to consider color, value, and print size. In Tuscany Bears all the bear claws are the same and the quilt is made from a relatively small number of fabrics, whereas Menopausal Bears (page 122) goes wild with over 60 fabrics. The sashing and border fabrics play a key role in unifying the design in these quilts.

MATERIALS FOR TUSCANY BEARS

Quilt size: 51" x 51" Block size: 12¼"

Materials	Yards
Assorted fabrics (mini-blocks)	scraps, less than ¼
Light orange (mini-blocks, pieced setting triangles)	¼
Green (mini-blocks, pieced setting triangles)	½
Yellow (blocks, border)	⅔
Blue (blocks)	⅓
Light stripe (blocks)	¼
Bright orange (cornerstones)	¼
Large Tuscany print (mini-blocks, setting triangles, corners, outer border)	1½
Small Tuscany print (mini-blocks, sashing strips, border)	¾
Small Tuscany print (binding)	½
Batting 54" x 54"	
Backing 54" x 54"	

The quilt has 20 mini-blocks, two of each, in the five Bear's Paw blocks. Choose any mini-blocks and arrange them as desired. For example, pair like mini-blocks together or make four each of five kinds.

CUTTING FOR INDIVIDUAL MINI-BLOCKS

Note: Size of mini-block is 4" unfinished. Four needed for each block. Five blocks, total of 20 mini-blocks.
Optional: Use more than two fabrics in mini-block. For piecing instructions see page 98.

Mini-block	Fabric A	Fabric B
Traditional Bear's Paw	(1) 4" square	
Square-on-point	(1) 4" square	(4) 2¼" squares
Bowtie	(2) 2¼" squares	(2) 2¼" squares
	(2) 1¼" squares	
Spools	(2) 2¼" squares	(1) 2¾" square
	(1) 2¾" square	
Pinwheels or Broken Dishes	(2) 2¾" squares	(2) 2¾" squares
Birds of the Air	(1) 2¼" square	(1) 2⅝" square cut in half diagonally
	(1) 4⅜" cut in half diagonally	
Sawtooth Star	(1) 2¼" square	(4) 1⅜" square
	(8) 1⅜" squares	(4) 2¼" x 1⅜"
Puss-in-the-Corner	(1) 2¼" square	(4) 2¼" x 1⅜"
	(4) 1⅜" squares	
16-patch	(2) 1⅜" x 7"	(2) 1⅜" x 7"
Wedge	(1) 4" square	(2) 2¼" x 4"
		(1) 2¼" square

CUTTING FOR TUSCANY BEARS

5 blocks

Mini-block	Fabric	Size
20 mini-blocks; Assorted fabrics; see page 119.		
Bear claws	Blue	(40) 2¾" squares from (3) full-width strips
Bear claws	Yellow	(40) 2¾" squares from (3) full-width strips
Center squares	Orange	(5) 2¼" squares (Optional: Fussy cut)
Rectangles	Stripe	(20) 2¼" x 5¾" (Optional: Manipulate direction of stripes)
Corner squares	Yellow	(20) 2¼" squares
Sashing		
Sashing strips	Small Tuscany	(16) 2¼" x 12¾"
Cornerstones	Orange	(4) 2¼" squares (Optional: Fussy cut)
Triangular cornerstones	Orange	(3) 3¾" squares cut diagonally both ways (Optional: Fussy cut)
Pieced setting triangles and corners		
Rectangles	Light orange	(8) 2¼" x 5¾"
Triangles	Green	(2) 8¾" squares cut diagonally both ways
Squares	Large Tuscany	(4) 5¾" squares (Optional: Fussy cut)
Corners	Large Tuscany	(2) 9½" squares cut in half diagonally
Borders Note: Before cutting, measure center field; adjust length of border strips, if necessary.		
First and third borders	Yellow	(8) 1" x 40½"
Second border	Small Tuscany	(4) 1½" x 40½"
Border corners	Orange	(4) 1½" squares (Optional: Fussy cut)
Border corners	Yellow	(8) 1" x 1½", (8) 1" x 2½"
Outer border	Small Tuscany	(8) 1½" x 4"
Outer border	Yellow	(16) 1" x 4"
Outer border	Large Tuscany	(4) 4" x 40½" (Optional: Cut longer initially to adjust print position)
Outer border corners	Large Tuscany	(4) 4" squares (Optional: Fussy cut)

Constructing Tuscany Bears

1 Make 20 mini-blocks of your choice (see page 98). Assemble the five Bear's Paw blocks (see pages 93-95).

2 Lay out the blocks and components of the center field in the desired configuration.

3 Construct the pieced setting triangles. Join a light orange rectangle to one side of each 5¾" square. Add the orange triangles to the remaining light orange rectangles, then join these to the 5¾" squares. If the squares were fussy cut or have a large print, pay attention to the orientation so that you sew the rectangles onto the correct sides. Add the green triangles.

4 Assemble the blocks, sashing strips and cornerstones, pieced setting triangles and corners in diagonal rows (see pages 27-28).

5 Carefully trim the center field so that there is an even ¼" seam allowance on each side (see page 28). There will be very little to trim and the corner triangles are exactly the right size. It should measure 40½" x 40½" after trimming. Measure yours and adjust the size of the border strips, if necessary.

6 Add the borders. Begin by joining the yellow first and third borders and Tuscany small print second border 40½" strips. Frame the orange squares with the short yellow strips: Sew the 1½" strips on opposite sides then add the 2½" strips. Add these to each end of the top and bottom borders. Attach the side borders and then the top and bottom borders to the quilt. Take care to align the narrow yellow strips at the seams before sewing in place.

Sew the outer border. Begin by sewing the yellow 1" x 4" strips onto the 4" sides of the eight 1½" x 4" Tuscany small print strips. Add one of these pieced sections to each end of the 4"-wide border. Sew the side borders onto the quilt top. For the top and bottom, add the corner squares and then join to complete the quilt top.

TIP: Cut the large print strips lengthwise and longer than necessary. This allows you to position the print so that the large flowers remain intact. Trim to the correct size.

7 Lay the quilt back flat, wrong side up, on a firm surface. Place the batting on top of the backing and smooth out. Layer the quilt top, right-side up, over the backing. Baste the layers and quilt as desired. Quilter Wanda Rains quilted an interlocking allover tulip pattern on Tuscany Bears.

8 Add the binding.

Take this pattern a step further: delve into your scrap stash to increase the numbers of fabrics and dramatically change the outcome. Menopausal Bears includes over 60 fabrics. The layout and size of the pieces are the same as for Tuscany Bears, apart from the mitered border.

Menopausal Bears made by the author (48" x 48")

After piecing the mini-blocks and bear claws, I was close to throwing this project away. I couldn't get the pieces to work together. The funky large floral print that appears in the setting triangles and corners was the theme fabric from which I coordinated the rest. I had to devise a way to salvage the project, and my best solution was to use a different pale color for the background in each block. The blocks took on a new look, and the black and hot pink sashing and border fabric made it a winning quilt. Menopausal Bears seems a fitting title for this taxing, irritable quilt made in my 50th year, which went from gloom and doom to fantastic!

Appendices

APPENDIX 1
TRIP AROUND THE WORLD BLOCK PATTERN FOR TOTE BAG

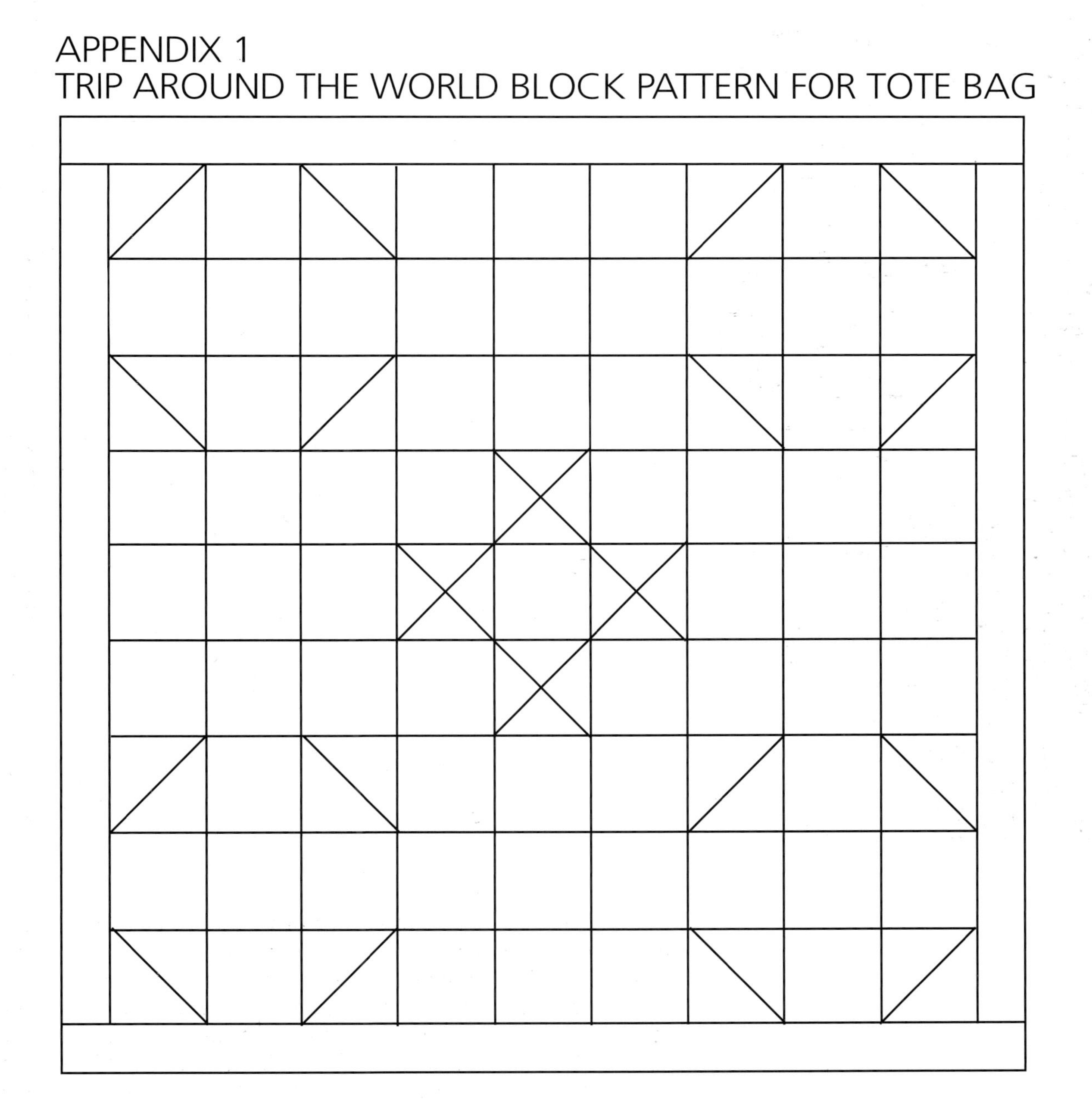

APPENDIX 2
WEEKEND TRIPPER PATTERN

APPENDIX 3
TWEAKED OHIO STAR 9-BLOCK SAMPLER PATTERN

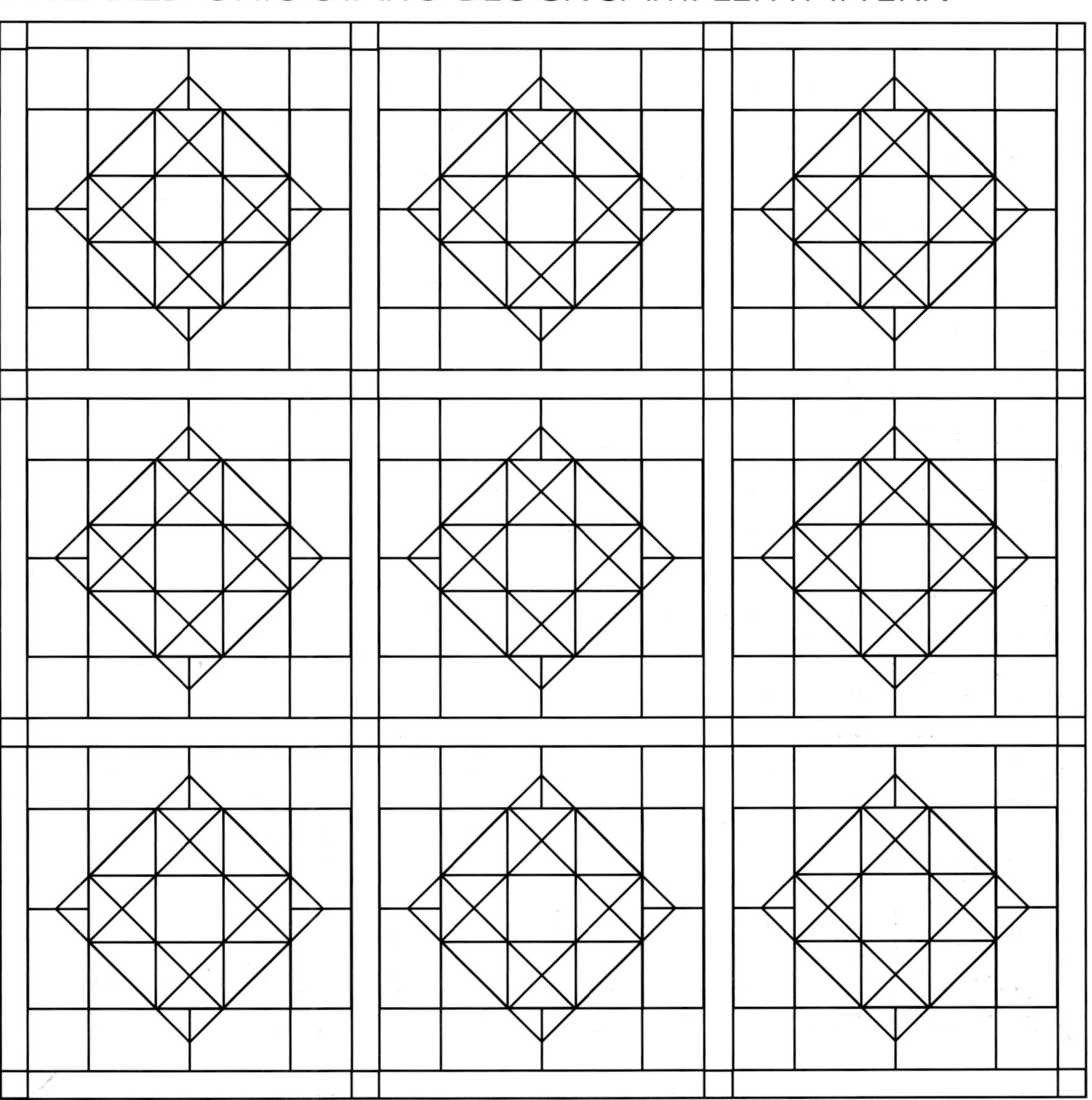

APPENDIX 4
TWEAKED OHIO STAR 9-BLOCK SAMPLER PLANNER

Example is the center block of "Stars at Sunset".

Block components	Cutting size	Example	Block 1	Block 2	Block 3	Block 4
Star points (¼-sq. triangles	(4) 3¾" squares	2 tan brown 1 yellow 1 orange				
½-sq. triangles	(4) 3½" squares	2 yellow 2 dark purple/blue				
Center square	(1) 3" square	dark purple/ blue				
Framing strips	(8) 2¾" x 4¼"	yellow				
Triangles for frames	(8) 1¾" squares	dark purple/ blue				
Outer corners	(4) 2¾" squares	orange				

Block components	Cutting size	Block 5	Block 6	Block 7	Block 8	Block 9
Star points (¼-sq. triangles	(4) 3¾" squares					
½-sq. triangles	(4) 3½" squares					
Center square	(1) 3" square					
Framing strips	(8) 2¾" x 4¼"					
Triangles for frames	(8) 1¾" squares					
Outer corners	(4) 2¾" squares					

Supply Sources

Antique Quilts
Joe and Mary Koval
Quilts and Antiques
Box 97
Schellsburg, PA 15559
(814) 733-0092
www.marykovalantiquequilts.com

Batting
The Warm Company
954 East Union Street
Seattle, WA 98122
(800) 234-WARM
www.warmcompany.com
Batting and pillow forms

Fairfield Processing
P.O. Box 1157
Danbury, CT 06813-1157
(800) 980-8000
www.poly-fil.com

Commercial Machine Quilting
Wanda Rains
Rainy Day Quilts
22448 N.E. Jefferson Point Road
Kingston, WA 98346
(360) 297-5115
www.rainydayquilts.com

Computer Software for Quilters
The Electric Quilt Company
419 Gould Street, Suite 2
Bowling Green, OH 43402-3047
(800) 356-4219
www.electricquilt.com

Decorative Threads
Sulky of America
P.O. Box 494129
Port Charlotte, FL 33949-4129
(800) 874-4115
www.sulky.com

Extension Tables for Sewing Machines
Dream World, Inc.
P.O. Box 89
Bonners Ferry, ID 83805
(800) 837-3261
www.dreamworld-inc.com

Fabric
David Textiles, Inc.
1920 S. Tubeway Avenue
City of Commerce, CA 90040
(800) 548-1818

Mats, Rotary Cutters and Rulers
Prym-Dritz Corporation
P.O. Box 5028
Spartanburg, SC 29304
(800) 845-4948
www.dritz.com

Mitering Ruler
Marti Michell
P.O. Box 80218
Atlanta, GA 30366
(800) 558-3568
www.frommarti.com

Quilt Photography
Mark Frey
P.O. Box 1596
Yelm, WA 98597
(360) 894-3591
www.markfreyphoto.com

Sewing Machines
VSM Sewing, Inc.
31000 Viking Parkway
Westlake, OH 44145
(800) 358-0001
www.husqvarnaviking.com

Threads
Coats and Clark
Consumer Services
P.O. Box 12229
Greenville, SC 29612-0229
(800) 648-1479
www.coatsandclark.com

Resources

Krause Publications
Publisher of this and other how-to books for quilting, sewing and other crafts
700 E. State St.
Iola, WI 54990-0001
(800) 258-0929
BooksCustomerService@fwpubs.com
www.krause.com

Clotilde LLC
P.O. Box 7500
Big Sandy, TX 75755-7500
(800) 772-2891
www.clotilde.com

Connecting Threads
P.O. Box 870760
Vancouver, WA 98687-7760
(800) 574-6454

Keepsake Quilting
Route 25
P.O. Box 1618
Center Harbor, NH 03226-1618
(800) 438-5464
www.keepsakequilting.com

Nancy's Notions
333 Beichl Ave.
P.O. Box 683
Beaver Dam, WI 53916-0683
(800) 833-0690
www.nancysnotions.com

Home Sew
P.O. Box 4099
Bethlehem, PA 18018-0099
(800) 344-4739
www.homesew.com

Herrschners Inc.
2800 Hoover Road
Stevens Point, WI 54481
(800) 441-0838
www.herrschners.com

About the Author

Maggie Ball has 20 years of quilting experience. Her award-winning quilts have been exhibited both nationally and internationally. She's a quilt show judge certified by the Northern California Quilt Council. She teaches quilting and traveled to Mongolia as a volunteer to teach unemployed and low-income women. Maggie has published two other books with Krause Publications, *Creative Quilting with Kids* and *Patchwork and Quilting with Kids*. A native of England, Maggie lives with her family on Bainbridge Island in the Pacific Northwest. Visit Maggie's Web site: www.dragonflyquilts.com.